British Wild Boar

The story so far

Derek Harman

Published in 2013 by Skycat Publications
Vaiseys Farm, Brent Eleigh, Suffolk CO10 9 PA
ISBN 978 0 9575673 2 0

Digitally printed by Book Printing UK
Remus House, Coltsfoot Drive, Woodston, Peterborough PE2 9BF
Email: info@BookPrintingUK.com
Telephone: 01733 898102   Fax: 01733 313524

© 2013 Derek Harman

This book is dedicated to all the people who encouraged me when the going got tough.

Without their help it would not have happened.

Acknowledgements

With grateful thanks to Frank and Lisa
for all their help in the research and
study period of this book.

To Peter for his guidance and patience,
and for his encouragement during those times when
my pen was reluctant to meet paper.

To Terry for his help and
advice in the layout of this book.

Contents

About the Author

I WAS BORN in October 1941 during the dark days of World War II, in a three bedroom cottage in Poundfield Road, Crowborough, a small town in East Sussex. My father was a Warrant Officer 2nd class in the Royal Army Medical Corp. I never knew him – he was killed six weeks before I was born. As so many during those troubled times, I was brought up by my mother with the help of aunts and grandparents.

My grandfather and uncle, I recall, spent all their spare time catching rabbits which were sold or exchanged at the local butchers. Sometimes for fresh meat and occasionally beef bones which went into the stew pot permanently deployed on the cast iron range. Beef bones went a lot further than rabbit and with vegetables provided an economic wholesome stew for the family for several days. This was a staple part of the diet for many during the war years and after. Rabbits were plentiful and relatively easy to come by living as we did on the edge of Ashdown Forest. It did become more difficult as time went on as more and more people tried to supplement their rations with rabbit. Further, large parts of the forest had been taken over by the military and were therefore officially closed to the public. But needs must and for those who knew where to look a steady supply of rabbits continued until the end of rationing. So it was grandad and uncle's pursuits that stirred my early interest in wildlife which became a life-long passion.

A move from Sussex to the North Downs of Kent in 1953 introduced me to game keeping. My stepfather had taken a job on a tenanted farm and came with a tied cottage. The keeper's son and I became close friends and I spent all my spare time, rain or shine, winter and summer helping the keeper with checking trap lines, feeding pheasants and running any errands. As a reward I was occasionally allowed to carry a .410 shotgun used to help control vermin such as magpies and jays. Left unchecked they could wreak damage to the game birds on the estate.

At school, I talked of little else but wildlife and country pursuits. So it came as no surprise to anyone, not least my career's officer despite his attempts to have me do otherwise, that I joined the gamekeeping trade when I left.

Derek Harman
April 2013

Introduction

LIVING AND WORKING on a farm in those days generally involved the whole family at busier times such as harvesting and thrashing. Indeed it was a condition of employment if the job came with a tied cottage as ours did. It was difficult to juggle my game keeping duties and help out on the farm but I managed. The local hunt was the Tickham and they hunted the estate twice a year after the shooting season ended. Their presence was not appreciated by the keepers because it meant that snares and traps had to be removed across the entire estate for each visit. Especially annoying at times when vermin control was the main priority in preparation for the nesting season. Nevertheless I enjoyed the spectacle of a well turned out hunt. My introduction to hunting came with the first Boxing Day meet after the war of the Eridge Hunt at Eridge Park. The whole family walked six miles to the meet. I remember my Grandfather pronouncing that the recommencing of this tradition was a sure sign that the hostilities of war were over. It heartened everyone to hear this. The meet was so crowded and bustled with activity. There was much jostling and the only way for us youngsters to see anything was sat on someone's shoulders. My fondest memory of that day was being lifted up onto a horse by one of the followers where I could see everything going on. It was such fun.

Life remained hard for everybody for a long while after the war. So much so that during harvest it was not unusual for the entire family to follow behind the binder to collect the ears of wheat left behind. Once the field was cleared, and with a nod from the farmer, we would take a sack or basket and pick up all the remaining ears – a task referred to as gleaning. If the crop had suffered wind or weather damage the number of ears left on the ground would be considerable and the farmer would have his own farm staff do the gleaning. We had to wait until they had finished before we were allowed onto the stubbles. It was a lot of effort for just a few bags of wheat ears but it was enough to help feed the chickens that most of us cottagers had at the bottom of our gardens. Competition was fierce for this valuable feed and it was not unusual for rival families to come to blows over a field of stubble. The rewards at stake were not great amounting to a half bushel of corn on an acre of ground. Even so, a stubble field of five or six acres was a welcome-enough opportunity when times were as hard as they were. All the while I toiled I was learning about the myriad and plentiful wildlife that was around in those days. Vast flocks of sparrows and finches were commonplace and our constant companions as we searched the fields, a sight that sadly is no more.

My interest in fishing came about quite by chance when I was about seven years old. I was helping an old lady with her garden in order to acquire my first bike; the deal was that I helped out with her garden and in return she would give me the nice "shiny" bike that was parked in the back of her garden shed. The bike used to belong to her son who sadly had been a victim of the final push to Berlin at the end of the war. It had been propped there unused since before D-Day. It was covered in dust and cobwebs, had a fixed gear drive and a puncture but to me it was a Rolls Royce of a bike. If pulling weeds in the flower beds, dead-heading the roses and scrubbing the red brick paths surrounding the house would get me that bike then I was all for it. It was a visitor to the house, a gentleman of advanced years, who got me interested in fishing. He owned a large house, some three miles away and in the grounds surrounding this very large property was a trout lake. It was in this lake that I caught my first fish with a rod loaned to me by the owner. Later this became my very own rod and being my first was one of my prized possessions for many years. I had an open invitation to fish this lake whenever I wished.

The one proviso was that I always call at the big house first to make sure no one else was fishing the lake that day. Aside from trout I was allowed to catch anything on the understanding that the catches were released into the outlet stream and not returned to the trout lake. To ensure that I did not catch any trout I was restricted to bread paste and flour and water bait. The owner always checked my bait to make sure I did not have any worms with me. I thought that to be a small price for a free day's fishing and I did not mind these restrictions at all. It was the solitude and the opportunity to study the wildlife that I relished most. I do recall being constantly nagged by the thought of what I would do if I accidently caught a trout and it was discovered because that would have been an end to my visits to this blissful lake?

Though no longer directly active in hunting, shooting and fishing I am as passionate as ever in countryside issues. I have a favourite saying, "a town dweller wakes up in the morning to a new day whilst a true countryman awakes and sees a new page". This I believe is what separates the genuine countryman from the casual countryside visitor be it for sport, pleasure or whatever.

So as the first reports of "strange" creatures roaming the countryside reached me, it was my cue for a new page.

From the first sightings of "Big Cats" back in the early seventies through to the first sightings of wild boar in the late eighties. I was always a bit cautious about the big cat's at first and thought at the time that probably a liquid lunch or dinner may have a bearing on the information, how wrong I was! The evidence for big cats is overwhelming, proof for their existence can be found all over the country; if you talk to people who know and not those who think they know. The only thing lacking is a clear, distinct picture. The evidence for the boar is now a matter of record.

My first encounter with a wild boar occurred soon after they escaped into the countryside in the late eighties and, along with others, I reported my sighting to the "Powers that Be". My attempt to inform was dismissed as just another "Beast of

Bodmin" story despite the fact that many similar reports had been received. Undeterred I vowed to show my doubters that this was no figment of my imagination and that there really were wild boar roaming our British countryside.

Twenty years on and those experts who had earlier claimed that wild boar could not and would not survive in twentieth century Great Britain have feasted on a considerable amount of humble pie. Wild boar can take care of themselves perfectly well and indeed positively thrive in the countryside today, from Dover to Bodmin, Southampton to Scotland and all counties between.

It wasn't plain sailing, sometimes I was going nowhere and was about to give up but somebody was smiling down on me when I finally captured the first video footage of free living wild boar in the south east of England. Those first few minutes of footage now take pride of place in my collection of forty eight hours of wild boar video. Much of it has been used by several television production companies for programmes about wild boar. During the making of these programmes, I have been fortunate to have met a number of famous wildlife presenters. It is their encouragement, along with that of close friends that led me to write this book. In publishing my research and up-close experiences with these magnificent creatures, it is my aim to correct the misleading and inaccurate information that has been published and dispel the many myths concerning the free living wild boar in Britain today.

After twenty years of study and discovery, I have for the first time recognised I have been on a personal journey with wild boar as my constant companions. I started as a naïve novice and maybe as I put pen to paper I could consider myself an expert.

Well expert or not, for sure there is still much to learn about these animals and this book is most certainly not the final chapter in the life of wild boar in the UK.

The data included in this book has been collected by me personally over countless hours of observation and study of different family groups – sounders as they are known.

Welcome to My World

Chapter One

The Beginning

I T WAS a pleasant Sunday afternoon in late autumn 1989. My wife was visiting her mother and I was taking full advantage of her absence, lazing in front of a warm fire watching the sport on TV. Afternoon gave way to evening, and with cup of tea in hand and enjoying those dreamy thoughts only an open, blazing fire can induce, I was at ease with the world, oblivious to what was to come. My wife returned later that evening, I turned as she walked through the door to see a look of concern directed my way. Clearly gathering her thoughts a second or so passed and then, "I've just seen a pig in the road just outside the village," she exclaimed.

"Couldn't have been. No one rears pigs around here. Probably a dog or something," I retorted, dismissively.

"Not a farm pig, a big black hairy one," she replied sharply, "Like those you see in nature books."

Somewhat taken aback by her prickliness and there being no obvious signs that her father's cider had been at work, I suggested that she show me where she had seen this black beast. A confident, "I'll show you" nod she turned, opened the front door leaving it open for me to follow. We jumped in the car and drove to the spot outside the village where she had seen the animal. Nothing.

"There you are, told you so." Smugness written all over my face.

"I know what I saw. It was a big black thing with long black hair," she replied with conviction.

Realising that she was not going to change her mind, I took a spotlight out of the car and began a sweep across the fields on each side of the road. The first pass revealed nothing. I turned the light toward the field on the opposite side of the road. To my utter amazement, there in the middle of the field was a large black boar! It took off as soon as the lamp found it.

My wife looked at me with one of those looks that said, "I told you so" and strode back to the car. After watching the boar disappear into the spinney on the far side of the field, I joined her. We travelled home in silence. I could almost feel her joy radiating from her as I drove. As soon as we got back, I telephoned the only boar farm within 50 miles to tell them one of their boars was on the loose. It was the done thing to report roaming livestock – unwritten country code. I didn't feel much like a good Samaritan when the grumpy voice at the other end implied I was an interfering ignorant townie.

"Our fences are sound and in any case our animals are a contented lot, they wouldn't want to escape. Probably a zoo escapee or from France swum across the Channel to mate with our sows," he suggested with a chuckle.

The guy was now obviously getting some pleasure from this attempt at humiliation. A polite "thank you we will look into it" would have satisfied me. But now my paddy was up, mickey-taking was one thing but being called a "townie" boiled me over.

"Look here, firstly I'm stone cold sober, secondly I haven't come up the river on a push bike and for your information I am a countryman born and bred. What I saw was a boar on the loose!" Having said my piece I paused and then politely said, "Goodbye and thank you for listening."

Over the next few days I asked around to see if anyone else had seen the boar. One local farmer had been chased from a field as he had gone to feed his sheep. The field was less than a mile away from where my wife and I had made our sighting. The farmer told his tale. By this time the animal I had seen had gained considerably in both height and weight, almost doubling in size in the last 24 hours. Having made due allowance for this individual's renown tendency to exaggerate, I concluded it had to be the same animal. He had also contacted the boar farm and had received a similar unhelpful response.

It would be another eight years before I saw my next live boar.

Following my first encounter, I started to hear about unexplained damage to pasture land, fences completely flattened and strange looking unidentified creatures seen fleetingly at night picked up in the headlights of cars. One lady was convinced she had seen a circus bear with the heavy set shoulders and shape of a miniature bison standing about 3 foot 6 inches high. It had a long nose and long, black, shaggy hair. It seemed certain to me from these reported sightings over the ensuing 18 months that there was more than one animal on the loose. Not even the Houdini-like wild boar could be in two places at once.

Outdoor pigs

Evidence came in 1991 when a farmer situated not more than four miles as the crow flies from my first sighting, went to feed his outdoor pigs, only to find a large black boar in the field chatting up one of his sows. The boar took exception to being disturbed and promptly charged the farmer who fortunately reacted quickly enough to avoid what would have been serious injury. The boar charged straight past the stack of timber upon which the farmer had taken refuge. It ploughed through the hedge as if not there, leapt through the ditch and into the next field. And there the excited boar waited, torn between the desire to return to the sow who stood waiting for him to finish what he had started and the chance to see off a potential threat. Passion won over and the boar returned to his conquest. The farmer, still a little shell shocked at the spectacle, quietly withdrew from his sanctuary leaving the boar to finish what he had started.

Upon his return home and a glass of courage later, he called a friend, a keen shooting man who immediately offered his services. The two men approached the field. The boar, now looking quite at home, once again took exception to the human presence. The creature made ready for a charge but instead he dropped to the ground in response to a well placed shot to the head. Both men looked incredulously at what lay before them. The animal was four years old or thereabouts and turned the scales at a touch over 300lbs (or 136kg in new money). The local press, which had shown little interest in the many tales of mystery sightings now had a photograph and proof that wild boar had returned to England. Armed with this juicy story, this time it was the press that the boar farm had to answer to.

Their response? A pregnant sow may have escaped during the storm of February 1989 which had brought down trees weakened in the great storm of 1987 and maybe breeched a fence. This admission raised a few eyebrows amongst the more knowing local farming community. The dates simply did not add up. This sow would have had to produce two year-old piglets and that would have made biological history. Patently there had either been escapes in 1987 or more than one animal had escaped in February 1989 or both.

Stories of damage to hop gardens, vineyards, agricultural crops, and pasture land were now being regularly reported by the press with attention grabbing headlines concerning lambs being killed and eaten. In actual fact remains comprised patches of blood and a couple of hooves and that was it. Nevertheless the evidence for several wild boar being out there was growing. Domestic pigs are bred to produce large litters, with litter sizes of eight or ten being typical, 12 to 14 was not unusual. A few simple calculations confirmed what those at the centre of animal husbandry were already thinking. If these wild boar on the loose produced piglets at the same rate their population could become a very serious issue. Action was needed but by who?

Some organisations chose to interpret these stories as just another ruse to raise awareness of the plight of the farming community. The NFU had little interest and they would not canvas the Ministry of Agriculture, Fisheries and Food, MAFF, until they had cast iron evidence that wild boar in number really were once again roaming the countryside of Britain after an absence of 400 years. They stood by their belief that the only boar on the loose had already been killed. End of problem. Proof for my thinking that after their escape, (or deliberate release as some conspiracy theorists thought), boar had quickly disappeared into the countryside was not going to be easy to come by.

Shy and secretive by nature they had become at home in the woods and forests of south east England, doing what boar do very well – avoiding contact with humans and building up a viable breeding population. Reverting to their secretive and nocturnal habits strengthened this endeavour. So, with my interest stimulated after the shooting of the four-year-old male in 1991, I set about following up leads and reported sightings but frustratingly they always turned out to be old news or cold trails. Typically I would hear, "a friend of mine saw one a couple of weeks ago on his way home from the pub, it crossed the road in front of his car and went off into the woods", or, "a farmer has had some pasture turned over in his fields by the forest", or "the dogs chased one out of a pond at the back of the farm buildings where we dump the waste produce" and so on. These sightings were more often than not relayed to me weeks, sometimes months after the event. I was always grateful for these snippets – any news is better than none but the dead ends were very frustrating. Undeterred, I spent all my spare time following up as many sightings as I could, talking to the people involved and looking for any tell-tale signs. Most often the signs were stale and by no means certain to be that of wild boar. Much turned out to be the work of badgers. Badgers root for worms and grubs in a similar manner to wild boar but once the two are seen in the same locality then the difference is quite obvious. Despite the time lag and resulting cold trails, I began to piece together data that pointed to potential habitats for our elusive immigrants.

Not one of us

The woodland around Aldington and Lyme in East Kent became a focal point and most of my time was spent in this part of the county. The press and TV became aware of my activities and wanted interviews. I was only too happy to oblige. Any publicity that would help to uncover the extent of the wild boar presence was most welcome. It was with this in mind that I attended a meeting of the local branch of the NFU as a guest of one of the members. At this stage in my research I was predicting a potential disaster. My life has revolved around farming and the countryside as it is today. I passionately believed that the last thing the farming industry needed were herds of wild pigs cutting swathes through the countryside. The prospect of disease and damage to crops and livestock on top of the prevailing economic woes was the farming community's worst nightmare. The threat to human beings and pets particularly dogs were a real possibility. The response to my request, a total snub, not one of us, you know. "If we have any information it will be passed to the appropriate department at the ministry not to an outsider" was the clear message.

Hunter's surprise

One day around this time, and with no prior warning, a picture of a hunter with a wild boar across his shoulders appeared in a national newspaper. The boar had been shot, so the paper reported, on an estate at Tenterden in Kent, in fact not very far from the very first sightings of boar and less than half a mile from the local boar farm. It was a young animal, not more than twelve months old and one of six found in a large patch of brambles in one of the woods on the estate during a vermin shoot. The beaters had no idea that the boar were there until the animals burst from cover, taking off in all directions. It must have been quite a sight. Twelve bore shotguns loaded with standard ammunition were the order of the day for vermin control. They were using BB, three, four and five-shot cartridges, ideal for foxes and smaller vermin but completely useless against wild boar. One member of the shoot however, was mistakenly using cartridges with heavier shot intended for long range goose shooting. He was able to stop one of these boar and this animal was the one receiving due recognition in the national paper albeit posthumously.

Once again the boar farm denied all knowledge. However, at the very time of these denials, a number of traps had appeared on the fence lines around the enclosure of the boar farm. Doubtless to try and catch some of these French females for his resident stock boar. Or maybe to recapture some of the returning boar desperate for the sanctuary the farm offered!

One week later it was decided to drive the same piece of wood again and this time I was present. Another animal was shot, a female weighing some 100lb (40-50kg). She was pregnant and would have given birth within a couple of weeks. She had three, more or less full grown piglets inside her. At last I had a chance to have a good look at one of these animals at close quarters. The first thing that struck me was that here was an animal that was not more than 12 months old and yet she was carrying young and about to give birth. The gestation period for pigs is three months, three weeks and three days. She had mated when she was just nine months old. Body weight is one determining factor in assessing the sexual maturity of pigs so she clearly had access to a plentiful supply of good food. Forty-five kg is the recognised weight for first time gilts, a gilt being the name given to first litter females; the gilt becomes a sow after she has weaned her first litter.

This reported episode further stimulated the growing intrigue within the locality. Now, everybody had a story to tell about an encounter with boar. Some involved road traffic accidents, farmers with fences damaged and so on. One farmer commented, "It was as though a bulldozer had gone through it".

9

By now it was quite clear that there had been one or more further escapes from the boar farm, this time in sizeable numbers both male and female of varying ages. More stories of lambs killed and eaten over the border in Sussex, hop gardens uprooted and pastures overturned. Road accidents involving wild boar became more frequent with some cars being write-offs. Fortunately no one had as yet been seriously injured. People described their unfortunate encounters, "They came out of nowhere and gave me no chance to brake", "It's quite a shock to the system to be suddenly confronted by several boar in front of the car", and "I now try to avoid driving round the lanes at night."

All at once wild boar meat was in demand and the local game dealers were paying good money for wild boar with no questions asked as to the origin of the carcass; poached or legal it made no difference as long as it was boar and fit for human consumption. There was no legislation in respect of hunting them. As far as the authorities were concerned wild boar did not exist. Their only mention was in the Dangerous Wild Animals Act, amended in 1986 to include wild boar after it became clear that wild boar farming was on the increase and the numbers were likely to increase as demand grew for boar meat, both farmed and, at that time, imported. In the mid-nineties there were wild boars for the taking if you could find them, and a ready demand for the flavourful meat.

Media interest was also on the rise; suddenly everyone wanted to know what was going on. Wild boar was big news. The media interest also stirred the ministry into life and they began to take a lot more interest in boar activity in Kent and East Sussex. At this stage they were motivated solely by the issues of public risk. Increasing reports of traffic accidents were a concern and they wanted to be seen to be on the case lest a serious injury or fatality should occur.

The man from the ministry
And so it was that one evening during this period of heightened interest from government, I received a phone call from a man at the ministry, at least that is how he announced himself.

He explained that he had been asked by the Central Science Laboratory to look into the claims that wild boar were roaming the Kent and East Sussex countryside causing damage to farmland and raising havoc with livestock. He had been given one month to undertake his nationwide investigation and to produce his report. He was aware of my interest and was keen to meet with me. Needless to say I was equally keen to participate in his study and agreed he should call on me the following evening. He was in for a surprise. I contacted several people I knew to have had encounters with wild boar in some way. Local game dealers who had been trading in boar carcasses for some time – one had a boar carcass currently hanging in his chillers and the man who shot the boar in 1991 after it had charged his neighbour were among those invited.

The following evening at 7.30pm precisely, a knock on the door heralded the arrival of the man from the ministry. I should confess, I expected to be greeted by a stuffy, 50-something gentleman, suited with collar and tie. The fellow before me was anything but; a student type in his twenties sporting long shoulder length black unkempt hair and more earrings than my wife had in her entire collection.

Pleasantries exchanged and refreshments dispensed, we got down to the main reason for his visit. Word had obviously spread further and faster than I had anticipated. Two of the individuals I had invited were on his list of people to see. Our man from the ministry listened intently to the accounts from those who'd had close encounters of various kinds, making copious notes as he did so. He studied the maps laid out on the table, taking note of each sighting and encounter as they were pointed out. No question, the man from "M" left with very much more data than he could have hoped for and more crucially all the proof he needed; wild boar were, in number, roaming the countryside of Kent and Sussex. The stories that had percolated through the farming authorities were not, after all, the imaginings of a few rustic rogues. The boar were for real.

Encouraged by this acquisition of knowledge and certain that he would need a lot more time to investigate, "M" returned to HQ and negotiated a revised study term of six months for his interim report. Courtship over, it was now down to business and he quickly realised he was in deep up to his neck. He knew nothing about wild boar, their feeding, breeding habits, food likes and dislikes, habitat preferences and so on. To cap it he had never seen a wild boar, not even a picture. He was expecting to be looking for a domestic pig gone wild. I offered to help, unofficially of course. My offer was duly accepted so long as his masters did not become aware. Help from the general public was frowned upon, not one of us you know.

This was in 1996/7, I had been studying boar activity in the area ever since my first sighting in 1989 so was well placed to help and in truth eager so to do. As well as passing on to him all the fresh information that I had uncovered, I also acted as go between, providing "M" with updates on sightings etc as it was passed to me. Country folk will talk quite openly to a fellow countryman but have an inbuilt reserve when it comes to those in authority.

Before too long however, it began to dawn on me that this had become a one way flow. A great deal of information went in to the ministry but little or nothing came out. Par for the course as government departments go I suppose. Despite the frustrating lack of feedback, I continued to follow up leads and was rewarded with my second live boar sighting, in fact two of them, a sow and a well grown youngster at foot. A colleague and I had been asked to investigate a new area of woodland when we surprised the sow who was rooting in a wet patch of ground on the edge of a large lake. She took off like a bat out of hell before the chap with me had a chance to get a clear shot. A missed opportunity to bag a wild boar but the find alone was a result as far as I was concerned.

Sometime later I took a call from a farmer who had some damage to a field of winter wheat. I met the farmer and together we walked the field. In several places the soil had been turned over. The footprints nearby indicated a large animal had been at work. The crop had been pushed aside but was otherwise untouched. What was the animal after? The farmer informed me that last year's crop had been fodder maize which had been cut in the autumn to make silage for the dairy herd. The boar was rooting for the cobs of corn that had been ploughed in during the autumn. I was keen to get a look at this animal and the farmer was keen to see the back of it. So my marksman friend and I set up camp with the aim of bringing the offender to book. Several wasted nights later we had an opportunity to use our new night vision equipment. We found a spot by a hedge with a good view of the area where the boar had recently been active and waited. Two and a half hours later whilst scanning with the scope, I spotted the boar, its blinking eye the give away. Our quarry had arrived on the scene. This was when I first noted that wild boar blink repeatedly every few seconds. We were down wind and from it's demeanour it sensed no danger. A boar's eyesight is very poor but this is compensated by excellent hearing and sense of smell. The fairly stiff breeze and our down wind approach kept our scent from the boar. A careful stalk got us to within sixty metres (60 yards) of the animal. A well placed shot to the head put him down, permanently. He was big and a tractor and front end loader came to the rescue. The farm buildings were about three-quarters of a mile away where there was sufficient light for us to ready the carcass for sale.

He was about four to five years old and had been in excellent condition with a thick coat of long black hair. He weighed in at a touch less than 145 kilos (320lbs). The following morning we photographed him for our records. The press soon arrived having been tipped off by the farmer the night before and they were taking their pictures as our man from the ministry arrived. It was his first opportunity to examine a fully grown male at close quarters and quite excited he was too. The boar was then shipped off to the game dealer for processing and after a 10 to 14 day hanging period sold to the general public.

Boar in the pond

And then there was the boar that fell in the pond. We had found signs of boar on farm land just outside Appledore and close to a picnic site. The foot prints were the largest we had found to date. This would be some boar. So, with the landowner's permission we placed feed by a large pond where tracks and mud patches provided the tell-tale signs that boar was using it to drink and wallow. After a couple of nights the boar found the feed and returned every night to clear up the food that the other wildlife had left. As a general guide if the boar return to a feed site three nights running then they are probably resident, if not then they will be nomads. Our food was expressly for the purpose of tempting the boar to present itself as a target but of course the badgers, foxes, deer and myriad birds, oblivious to our intent took advantage of a free meal any time it presented itself. The boar had returned three nights in a row and it was time we set up for him. We found a discrete position to observe the feed site, confident we would remain undetected by our intended victim and providing a clear and safe point to shoot from. This put us some 60 metres from the target zone right in the middle of a corn field. The night was moonless and pitch black. We set up our night vision gear and the separate infra-red light source, a necessary addition in those days. We waited and waited. Three hours had passed and my colleague was on the point of calling it a night when we heard a loud cough from the direction of the conifer plantation on the far side of the pond. A sure sign of large boar. The coughing sound made by a boar is a sure sign it is in a state of unease. It may have caught a scent it associates with danger, eg humans or maybe heard something unusual in it's proximity. There was a gentle breeze and this was coming from the conifer wood towards us so we were confident we were not the source of his anxiety. The sound ceased and a few moments later, I glimpsed movement out of the corner of my eye.

The large boar we had been patiently waiting for had emerged from the wood and stood at its edge some 100 metres away. It stood there almost motionless apart from lifting its head to scent the air. It surveyed the area for what must have been 10 minutes before finally stepping out onto the headland of the field and then immediately broke into a fast trot down to the feed site whereupon and without further ado its head went down and it began its evening meal. "Don't drop him in the pond," I whispered, "I don't fancy a midnight swim to get him out." Rifle at the ready, my colleague returned a "trust me, I'm a pro" look. He shuffled for position, took aim on the boar and pulled the trigger. The boar went down instantly, kicked once and promptly jumped straight in the pond! I think I must have said something like "Oh bother, Now what do we do?" My colleague may have a different recollection.

So we had a full grown brute of a boar stuck in the pond which we could not get to without a soaking and even if we were foolish enough to try we wouldn't be able to drag him any further than the edge of the pond. So when in trouble, phone a friend. Fifteen minutes later armed with a tractor and front loader, we lifted the boar on to dry land. Mission accomplished.

Within a couple of days of the pond incident I had a phone call from an artist in Cornwall who was trying to get hold of a boar skin for her work, I assume for the long bristles with which to make paint brushes. Now boar skin is usually surplus to requirements so we agreed to send the skin of the boar in the pond by carrier provided that she paid the postage. She willingly agreed until that is, we told her the skin tipped the scales at 52lbs.

Night of the wolves

My next encounter is one that raises the hairs on the back of my neck to this day despite the incident occurring several years ago.

Once again it was reported damage to a permanent pasture field some 100 yards from the edge of woodland and a request from the landowner for us to take a look. He thought it was badgers but was unsure. We had clear instructions that if we found boar, they were to be dealt with. This grassland, comprising about half an acre, had been turned over extensively and the level of destruction was far in excess of anything a badger could manage.

The wood in question had at its heart a large lake and it was on the edge of this lake that we set up our feeding site to try to draw the boar out into open ground where we could more easily fulfil the landowner's request. A bag of whole maize was suitably deployed at a site on the dam of the lake where it could be monitored from a discreet distance. A week of patient dusk and night surveillance yielded nothing. The food remained pretty much untouched save for that consumed by a few badgers who visited every night, grateful for the supplement to their regular diet. At the end of an unsatisfying week and close to drawing stumps, we decided to give it one more go; if we had no luck this time we would abandon the idea. On our final evening's watch, we arrived on site at dusk and once again got ourselves comfortable, readied for another long wait. After about two hours of nothing but the usual sounds of the night in a wood, there was a sudden loud crack of twigs snapping in the thicket on the far side of the feed site. Our spotlight, fitted with a red filter, revealed the head of a large boar peering from the brambles. Its attention firmly fixed on the feed site; it remained statue-like for about 10 minutes with two blinking eyes in the infra-red light the only give away that it was alive. Satisfied that it was safe to proceed, it cautiously moved into the open toward the source of food. It fell to a single shot. It was only as we approached the fallen beast that we realized the true size of this animal. The ground around the feed site was very soft and slippery underfoot and it quickly dawned on us that we would not be able to move it without help. It was now close to midnight. Despite the late hour, my companion went to the farm to seek assistance leaving me to sit and wait with the equipment and our trophy.

The farmhouse was about a mile and a quarter away, through rough and wooded ground so I did not expect to see anyone for quite some time. I made myself comfortable. Once more the myriad night dwellers, having been rudely awakened by the crack of the rifle, settled down. Owls and other nocturnal creatures resumed their hunting whilst the remainder snuggled up for the rest of the night. Then the temperature changed, and the wood suddenly fell silent again, the mist began to rise from the lake. As though on queue the wolves at the local zoo park started to howl. It sounded to me as I sat in this eerie wood in the middle of the night, as if the wolves were in the wood all around me. It sounded like a score or more of the beasts were contributing to this incessant cacophony and what was worse they seemed to be coming nearer. It was then that I saw the second boar appear on the far side of the feed site. It looked even bigger than the first. I picked up the rifle just in case the boar gave me a chance of a shot. My heart sank as I discovered the magazine had been removed. No ammunition in sight, I was rapidly trying to think through plan B, looking for the nearest tree , when I heard the sound of a tractor approaching as did the second boar. It disappeared without a sound. We pulled the carcass out of the bog with a long rope fixed to the tractor. It didn't take long and soon we had it on the scales. It was a touch over 300lbs cleaned.

The barbecue boar

The novelty of wild boar meat had raised demand significantly and with it the level of poaching to cash in on this public appetite. One story which I heard first hand I will retell here. However, for reasons that will become clear, the players shall remain anonymous. A local chap connected to the shooting industry was enjoying a beer in the pub one evening with a few like-minded people when the subject of wild boar came up. After discussing the merits or otherwise of boar as a quarry, this chap was asked if he could supply a wild boar for a family barbecue. Now a cautious, "I'll see what's about and get back to you" would have worked just fine but the request had come late in the evening. A couple of pints of ale and a polite request turned to a challenge. "No problem. I'll get it sorted tomorrow" he confidently pledges. Now the proposed family get together was a few weeks off so there should have been no problem. Oh dear, he tried all his sources and no boar anywhere. Mindful of his public commitment he was not about to go back and lose face. After some deliberation, he decided the only way out of this self-created predicament was to raid the local boar farm.

And so one moonless night, he and two pals were sat in a vehicle parked on a main road about a mile from the boar enclosure. Our pub man and one of his friends readied themselves for their sortie to the enclosure. The third man was to remain with the vehicle to act as lookout. The occupied farm buildings were a mile further on from the enclosure and so they felt very confident they could execute their mission undetected. A two-mile round trip if all went to plan. The return leg with a hefty boar necessitated some motorised transport and a quad bike was the order of the day. The two parties would stay in touch using two-way radios. The lookout would wait with the four-wheel drive vehicle, out of sight of the main road, ready to move in as soon as the boar was located, shot and moved back to the road. There the two men, bike and boar would be picked up and on their way before anyone noticed. Well best laid plans ...

It didn't quite turn out like this. It took a while to locate a boar in the enclosure in the first place and the main fence stood six foot high and was partly electrified. Further they had not anticipated just how dark it would be in the pen; they had ruled out the use of a torch. It was pitch black and progress was slow. After some three-quarters of an hour of staggering about in the mud, they resorted to using a pen light and targeted a boar that looked about the right size for a barbecue. They wasted no further time and promptly shot the boar using a gun with a silencer.

Things now going their way, they called in a status report to their mate at the pick-up and telling him to be ready for their return in about another half hour. The look-out was a little bemused when he received a call a few minutes later with a revised estimate for their return. When the two had gone to retrieve the shot boar it turned out not to be the 40 to 50kg they had at first thought. At the same time it became clear why they had been able to get close to this animal when all the others had moved away as they approached the pen. He was the dominant animal and would not back down for anything. Further they had not realised that the animal had not been standing up but was lying in a deep mud hole and so was much bigger – in fact a full grown adult about 145kg! It was going to take some time to get it back to the vehicle always assuming they could extract it from the deep mud holding it fast. After a few frantic failed attempts to shift it, they decided the only course of action was to reduce the dead weight. The look-out unexpectedly, and not without adding operational risk, changed to the role of logistics and ferried a knife to the pen to enable the head and feet of the enormous beast to be removed. Having no desire to remain a moment longer than necessary, he swiftly returned to his post. Eventually the now lighter carcass was moved to the side of the pen.

By now this activity had alarmed the other animals in the enclosure, all 200 of them. The two men were now feeling decidedly uncomfortable surrounded by an entire herd of wild boar. They knew well enough just what damage one anxious boar was capable of. Here was a veritable army and they sounded unhappy. The two men still had the six foot fence to negotiate with the carcass. The fence as well as being high and appearing higher by the second was on their radar but what they had neglected was the electrified wire that ran along the base of the fence, a foot high and a foot in front until that is one of them brushed it. The shock stunned him for an instant and he dropped his end of the boar. The boar fell onto the electric fence and with no malice on the part of the animal, instantly shared the electricity with the second man. He instinctively released the boar so that it now lay straddled across the fence. Every time they tried to move it they received another shock. By this time the lookout, becoming anxious, broke the radio silence protocol and called in. The call he felt was justified as the job which was to have taken one hour had now been running for three and a half hours and with no end in sight. He received his update and feeling the better for knowing of his colleagues' predicament, settled back down in the comfort of the vehicle.

The two poachers, after a few more mule kicks, extricated the boar from the live fence. They now had only the six foot fence to scale which, after a few more cuts, curses and bruises they managed. The one hour job had taken just over four and a half hours. There was the gutting and skinning to do before they could call it a night so by the time they got home it was daylight. All three were expected at work by eight o'clock!

The planned BBQ went ahead but to add insult to injury our unfortunate poachers were told the boar was rather tough and strong flavoured. The guests at the barbecue could not see what all the fuss was about as far as boar meat was concerned. If only they knew.

As I said, this story came straight from the horses mouth. I saw the result of their (miss) adventure hanging on the hook ready for the barbecue. Many a good poaching story gets frills added as it does the rounds. This particular one happened as writ.

There was a particular time when our man from the ministry found wherever he went he had an entourage. It was a perfect way to locate your next quarry. He was followed from one boar site to the next – a proper cat and mouse game. He would try to shake them off which would be met with devious counter measures such as change of cars when they thought they had been spotted. He would sometimes resort to using his ministry status – a flash of his pass at the local police station soon had the offender picked up on one charge or other and before too long the problem disappeared. Around this time 4x4 vehicles were frequently spotted cruising round the lanes after dark with a rifle poking out of the window. Many boar were killed by this means. The meat so obtained by-passed human consumption checks finding its way to local pubs and restaurants, game dealers and butchers. That was in the mid-nineties and, as far as inspection of carcases is concerned, nothing has changed.

Reputable game dealers do operate a strict code of practice as far as the care and sale of game is concerned and ensure they know the source and history of their purchases. Their business depended on trust and integrity. Poaching is similarly unchanged. Many still make a good living supplying both boar and venison to the grey market – a market that will prevail as long as there are those short of a few bob and happy to acquire cheap meat. A myriad of devices were deployed to catch a "boar for the pot", including snares which are illegal for deer but since wild boar "did not exist" as far as the law was concerned anything went. It was left to responsible-minded folk to remove and destroy these dastardly devices when we came upon them. More about this later.

The great storm 1987

So let's return to the question of just how these wild boar have returned to rural England. In the seventies and early eighties farming was going through a fairly difficult time and farmers needed innovative ways of making farming profitable once again. Increased efficiency was one sure way but was reaching natural limits. Diversification was another. What use could be made of hitherto unproductive areas of land? Raising wild boar was one such possibility. The first wild boar farms appeared in the mid-eighties. The breeding stock was purchased from private collections but in some cases surplus stock from zoos. A number of farms came together to form the British Wild Boar Association and by the late eighties/early nineties there were about 30 members. However, there were considerably more unaffiliated boar farms. The Great Storm of 1987 cut across south-east England bringing down thousands upon thousands of trees, devastating the countryside. Trees came down and took with them fences and inevitably some of these comprised the wild boar enclosures. If any boar escaped at this time it was not reported. A further less severe storm in February 1989 brought down more trees, mostly those weakened by the Great Storm two years earlier and more boar found their freedom.

The rapid increase in boar farms led to legislation which required those intending to raise boar to first obtain a "dangerous wild animal" licence before any boar could be brought onto the property. This licence also applies to cross-bred animals, so any wild boar cross is subject to the same level of control. The local council was given powers to police this licensing. There was little or no national guidance on how this should be managed and inevitably each council established their own set of rules and conditions, eg precautions and standards for boar herd security. Many local authorities failed to effect proper standards for fencing for example. Boar farmers were therefore free to use cheaper stock fencing intended for sheep and cattle, fencing that was no match for the power and tenacity of wild boar and escapes continued. Most of these escapes were not reported to the licensing authority as this would mean closure until a security measures inspection had taken place. We can be pretty sure that boar farms have been the main source of the free-living boar population in the countryside today with a little help from the deliberate release of some from private collections.

Time for a change

An event during the spring of 1998 would completely change my attitude to wild boar and be instrumental in heralding a new phase in my interest with wild boar. I was approached by a lady who owned some woodland adjacent to her garden. She knew that wild boar were frequenting her wood and had in fact caused some damage. Her main concern, however was that they may breach her fence and cause havoc in the garden. The fence was of light construction and a determined boar would have no difficulty breaching it. Having unsuccessfully tried various ways to deter the boar, it was time for more drastic action. We had to take down an animal in order to scare the rest away from the wood. Our intention was always to target an adult male.

There was always the risk of a misplaced shot – piglets without maternal support would not survive so females were avoided.

As ever, we had to wait until light had fallen and eventually the sounder arrived. A suitable target was selected and taken down with a single shot. When we got to the animal to my dismay we found it was a young female. Further examination showed that she was not feeding youngsters so there was no possibility of leaving piglets to starve which was a relief. I was, though still feeling down. This was the first sow we had shot. Still, what was done was done. The animal needed to be cleaned and quickly removed for chilling and butchering. When I opened her up my heart sank. She was carrying six piglets and was within a week or two of giving birth. I had been instrumental in the death of a pregnant female and her soon to be six young.

It was a Road to Damascus moment for me. There and then and for the rest of my life I would engage with wild boar constructively and supportively. For the very first time, I felt feelings of admiration for this wild creature that was re-establishing its presence despite the persecution from its human neighbours. I had been one such persecutor for the past seven years. That was now over. And so started my research, initial curiosity quickly became an obsession. The gun was now eagerly replaced by the camera and the pen!

Chapter Two

Change of Tactics

WE IN Britain have been out of touch with the activities of wild boar since that last one was killed back in the 1680s. Knowledge passed down by our forefathers through generation after generation has broken. No boar meant there was nothing to pass on. We are running blind and having to learn from scratch. Throw a heap of feed down and sooner or later you will get your boar provided they were there in the first place. But all that teaches us is that boar get hungry and, having once found a source of food, will continue to come to visit until the food source is exhausted or until they find a source in a safer spot or until they are shot. This teaches us nothing about the structure of the herd or sounder as it is known. We remain ignorant of their habits. We need to relearn all that we have lost and to do that we must observe and study them in depth. To uncover the mystery and restore our knowledge of these creatures requires time and effort, only then can we match the understanding and appreciation our forebears had of and for these ancient animals.

So where to begin? Chasing around the countryside looking at stale signs was informative but achieved very little other than to confirm what I already knew. A more scientific approach, that was what was needed, whatever that was. I come from a farming background. Country sports like hunting, shooting and fishing have given me an insight into the ways of wildlife. Game keeping taught me how to read the signs of the countryside. Husbandry of cattle, sheep, pigs and the like had given me an insight into the minds of animals. First and foremost they do not do anything without good reason. All animals have the same basic instincts, feeding to survive, fighting to achieve or maintain status in the herd or flock, and reproducing to pass on their genes. Wild boar have the same instincts but with different priorities. They (the males) once mature, put a good fight at the top of their list of things to do especially if it means showing off in front of the females! Just like Friday night down the pub really.

So the first step in my research was to find an area of woodland quiet and off the beaten track used by wild boar as a refuge. To pick a suitable location to set up an observation post away from prying eyes in order to observe without being observed and then wait and see what happened. Well, at first what happened was nothing. Plainly this was not going to work, the boar did not want to come out to play. No one had told them that I wanted to interview them. So plan B then. Find a recent rooting spot with some cover for a hide at a reasonable distance, put some feed down and wait for them to be tempted into the open. I found such a disturbed area by a clearing ride at Blacklands Wood in East Sussex. The ground had been turned over in a way that could only be the work of wild boar and, from the look of it, there was more than one animal involved. The perfect spot or so I thought. I laid down feed on the freshly turned area to see if the boar returned.

Taking the bait

The first night's food was gone the next morning and boar had taken the bait. But they were not the only creatures to take advantage of my hospitality. There were also signs of badger, fox, pheasant and other winged visitors. This was going to be more difficult than I at first thought. I was more than happy to feed the boar but not overly keen on my hard earned money providing every other head of wildlife with a three-course meal. Lesson learnt, the next lot of food went down at dusk when most other creatures were settling down for the night and this time was buried in the loose soil left by the boar the night before. This time the visitors were as I had hoped, wild boar. The ground had been freshly turned to a depth of about four inches and every grain of whole maize had gone. Feeling rather pleased with myself, I did the same the following night and waited in an area well away from the food in the hope of seeing the boar when they came to feed. After about an hour dusk gave way to night and it became too dark to see the feed site. Once again I left disappointed.

I went home wondering why they had not shown-up. Had they moved on or had something disturbed them? Well, the food was down and covered over as before so I just had to be patient and see what happened overnight. My visit the following evening found the ground disturbed over a wider area than before and my offering had once again been thoroughly appreciated. So, it would seem the boar were taking dinner after dark. This was no real surprise. I had found whilst involved with hunting boar that they were largely nocturnal mainly coming out of hiding after dark. I set down more food, waited until after dark then left for home and a nice cup of tea.

So, my routine for the next few days was finishing work at five, go home to collect the feed, drive out to the forest to check last evening's action, put down more food, stay on until dark, drive home and sleep. The boar, perhaps dubious of my company, were coming every night to feed but always after I had left. I could not believe that after 10 days I had not seen a single boar. It was clearly not going to be as straight forward as I first thought. Frustrating certainly, but deep down I was sure my persistence would pay off if I just gave it time. I just needed to be patient. This was the only way I was going to get to photograph free living wild boar.

My trusty Pentax fitted with a zoom lens and armed with 35mm film accompanied me each night. As the light faded though so did the possibility of my first photo. My Pentax was not designed for nocturnal ventures so I decided to invest in a video camera, resetting my sights on my first wild boar movie. A movie to convince the sceptics.

At the time there were plenty of special offers on video cameras. With prices greatly reduced it seemed to be the perfect time to buy. I had re-armed with a Sony Hi 8 handy-cam, which I was assured by the dealer was the bees knees and would do all I wanted it to. A few weeks later I found out why the camera had been on special offer. There was a new super duper model which could take moving pictures at night which was about to come onto the market. It was just what I needed but I could not afford the new model and had to make do with the one I had already purchased. I took it with me each time I went in search of wild boar sign. Perfect for recording scenes; I could study my finds in the comfort of my own home and replay them as often as I needed. An inspired decision if I do say so myself! My feeding routine continued at the same feeding area and three weeks passed but not a sign. Pleased as I was with my new technology I have to admit my initial enthusiasm was beginning to wane. But I continued to reason that it could only be a matter of time. Something deep within, an inexplicable belief, blind faith or sheer stubbornness, probably more of the latter, I cannot tell you. Whatever it was, a voice inside kept saying "Stay with it!"

Ten weeks and several pounds of maize later and with a pocket that was quite a bit lighter that inner voice had turned to a doubtful whisper. I recall getting home from work one evening at the end of one of those days when everything that could go wrong had done so. A day to forget and that called for a nice cup of tea. As I supped, I reflected on my dismal attempts to make film stars of my nocturnal friends. I was not feeling inclined to go to the feed site that evening. As I pondered whether it was time for a change of tactics, my wife who had been half listening to my bleating, out of the blue said, "Well you've been doing this for months now, you might just as well go and have a look. You can think about what to do next while you are there." Sounded good advice, I thought and promptly headed for the door, and turned to say something. "You might as well take that," she said, pointing to my video camera sat on the chair I had passed, "You never know what you might see."

First moving pictures of wild boar

I arrived at the woodland which now felt like my second home. I retrieved the food from the car boot, walked the 165 paces to the feeding site, set the maize down as I had done umpteen times before and returned to the car. From the car I had a clear view of one side of the feeding area. I sat and rolled a fag. I was about to light it when I caught sight of movement through the screen, a moving shape right there at the feeding site. I leaned forward, nose touching the screen and squinted; despite the fading light, there stood the unmistakable figure of a wild boar. I picked up the camera and with hands shaking began to film. At once I could see it was not alone. There were four, one male and three heavily pregnant females. The light was falling fast now but I resolved to keep the camera rolling. It was obvious from their demeanour they were uncomfortable out in the open without the security of complete darkness. One or more of the animals was constantly on watch for the slightest sign of danger and barked warnings at intervals. The rest of the group responded each time moving for cover at considerable speed only to return to the food a few moments later. I had no idea that these large animals could move so fast.

I stopped filming only when I and the camera could see no more. Now all I wanted to do was get home and replay what I had just witnessed. A celebratory drink was called for which as well as marking my long awaited sighting also steadied my still shaking hands enough for me to play the film on the television. Needless to say, I could not resist calling interested parties and before I had poured my second glass, the man from the ministry arrived, shortly followed by my shooting companion. It was now 10 o'clock but nobody, least of all me, cared a jot. The three of us knew this was a special moment. As I ran the film again, the man from M took notes. My colleague looked on in half-disbelief. He had only ever seen boar through the telescopic sights of his rifle. This was something else.

I now had the first video footage taken of free-living wild boar in the south-east of England, maybe the whole country. Now I had a chance to study these elusive and fascinating animals in the comfort of my own living room. All those hours, days and nights, those miles driving here, there and everywhere had finally paid off. It had all been worthwhile. Finally cracked it, right? Wrong. The following evening, I couldn't get to the site quick enough. I arrived well before dark, this time laying out double the feed, confident it would not go to waste and intent on persuading the boar to remain longer. My camera was now mounted on a tripod fixed to the car window. My generosity and greater preparedness did not, however, appear to impress the boar. They didn't come to feed any sooner, and, in the event, they did not come out to feed at all, at least not while I was there. I stayed until well after dark.

Disappointed, I drove home baffled as to why my previous evening's success had not been repeated. I had at least tested my new camera set-up and had discovered that the camera had a very sensitive built-in microphone. It had dutifully picked up every sound and I mean every sound, unravelling of sweet papers, clicking of cigarette lighter and even the squeaks made by me anxiously moving about in the car seat!

My ritual continued the following evening. Needless to say the site had been picked clean. The boar had returned, quite obviously after I had left for home. I fed the site, returned to the car, set up and waited. Almost at once the boar appeared in broad daylight, feeding on the freshly scattered feed, only three this time. The male was missing.

Caught off guard

Once again they had caught me out. The lens cap was still on and I was now to find out just how acute their hearing is. I moved as slowly and quietly as I could to remove the lens cap but just one squeak of the car seat and the boar took off so fast I saw only the back end of the last animal as it disappeared into the bushes. That was it for the night. I was kicking myself. My actors had arrived on cue, the stage was perfectly lit and the damned cameraman had left his lens cap in place. I would not make that mistake again.

The next evening, I laid the feed in full view on the same spot as before. My thinking, the resident pheasant population would be quick on the scene and, I hoped, their presence might subdue the boars' skittishness. It worked. The boar arrived just before it got dark. The three pregnant sows were in my field of view with just enough light to get a bit more film. When it was too dark to film, I stayed on for a while watching them using the night vision gear. The boar continued to clear up the remaining grains of maize, the pheasants having gone to bed long ago. The quiet of night was split by the loud exhaust of a passing land rover and that put the boar predictably, and in an instant to flight. Gone for the night.

A week passed before I saw boar again. This time just one, a single heavily pregnant sow who was so nervous. She spooked at the slightest sound. A small bird taking flight was enough for her to flee in a panic. She returned each time though and carried on feeding. I filmed her for some time until one chattering magpie was just too much for her and she left hot foot, this time for good. I continued to feed the site for three more days until food remained from the day before. A sure sign the boar had moved on.

Wild boar cross piglets

By now it was early summer, the woodlands were in full leaf, undergrowth was thick and many areas impenetrable. The ground was hard and dry and sign difficult to find. The boar sought out cooler and damper conditions. I was, once again, reliant on new leads. One would take me back to an area that I had visited before; the location where I had sat alone with just wolves, howling the night away, for company setting the hairs on my neck on-end as they did. Dog walkers had reported that their dogs were being chased by wild boar sows with well grown piglets at foot. These incidents took place on a footpath running along the edge of a field of linseed beside the wood with the lake at the far end. The crop had already been cut and the straw lay in rows across the field, providing good cover to observe the footpath and woodland. Maize deployed on the edge of the field, we settled behind a row of straw at the top of the field. No more than 10 minutes had passed when the boar emerged from the wood and began to feed. They were unusually carefree one might say almost bold. We had not expected a sighting and had little or no equipment with us. Crucially we had no rifle. My colleague crept away to retrieve a gun, leaving me to watch. The food consumed, the boar returned to the wood 10 minutes before my pal returned, much to his annoyance. These boar were exhibiting a good deal of bravado. On this form, maybe a further supply of feed may lure them out again. This we did and within five minutes out came the sows once more. If this was not enough to our amazement out from the wood came a stream of youngsters almost as big as their mothers. But there was something odd about these youngsters.

These were not your pure wild boar, they were cross bred with a domestic boar and bore his black colour. The sows were truly wild boar so at some point seven or eight months ago these sows had bumped into a black domestic boar from the farm next door. These cross bred piglets were the result of that encounter. There was no sign that the young were still being fed by the sows, indeed some of the youngsters looked old enough to breed themselves. Further, we were sure that the two adult sows were the dog-attacking culprits we had been seeking. The sows were taken out as requested of us and the youngsters returned to the farm next door where they were fattened up and sent to market a few weeks later. So I now had evidence that wild boar and domestic pigs can and do breed and by all accounts very successfully.

Late summer to early autumn is the most difficult time of the year for wild boar as far as their food supply is concerned. When the ground is hard and dry, rooting for earthworms and roots becomes difficult if not impossible. Further more, harvest is in full swing and the crops, used both as cover and food, are rapidly disappearing. As a result boar move back into the woods seeking out soft and boggy areas in which to forage. They will seek out dips and hollows and the wheel ruts left behind by the forestry operations over the years. These fill up with leaves which rot down to a fine leaf mould. These depressions in shaded areas remain damp and earthworms thrive on this mould so there is always something in the leaf litter for the boar to eat. Such foraging is time-consuming and dividends small but provides at least some sustenance until the oaks and chestnuts begin to drop their fruits.

Numbers and age

As the nights drew in it became more difficult for me to follow the activities of the boar. I worked six days a week and by the time I got home it was already too dark. In the black of night the boar would always be one step ahead of me. So, on Sundays, my one day off, I contented myself taking stock of the data I had accumulated, establishing the most likely places where the boar were laying up, estimating numbers, and age. The latter assessment came from taking careful note of footprint sizes. For boar up to about three years old, the size of the print correlates with age to a reasonable degree of accuracy. So the youngsters of that season will show up as much smaller footprints than, say, their mothers or aunts and uncles, who in turn would produce a print that was smaller than their mothers. Beyond about three years this means of age assessment is no longer reliable.

So locate the wet crossing places beside the tracks that criss-crossed the woods and start counting and measuring. You wouldn't stake your life on the numbers you come up with, but it puts you in the right ball park. Finding the crossing points also gave good clues as to where they were hanging out, providing valuable information for next year's feed sites.

It was while looking for wild boar sign that I had one of my closest encounters of the boar kind. I was visiting an area of woodland I hadn't been to in quite some while – a young conifer plantation comprising trees about 18 to 20 feet high which had not yet been thinned out. The undergrowth was thick and difficult to push through. I hadn't gone more than 20 yards, sorry, metres into the plantation when I detected the unmistakeable smell of a rutting boar. My immediate thought was that a boar must have passed this way recently and had probably urinated close by. I crouched down to look under the low branches of the fir trees seeking a path through the wood that was a little easier going than the one I had chosen.

The undergrowth comprised intertwined fir branches knitted together with brambles and honeysuckle. As I looked through this thicket, I saw, not more than 10 yards away a very large boar. I can say quite definitively that he did not much like being disturbed because without an instant's hesitation, he charged straight at me. Life-saving instincts, call it what you will, I don't remember making the leap but I found myself six feet from the ground, desperately clinging to the rather thin branches of a fir tree. The boar flashed by right underneath me and into the undergrowth where he stopped for a few minutes. He surveyed the surroundings looking for the intruder. I on the other hand, stayed exactly where I had found myself, muscles straining, not daring to move in case the flimsy branches that I was perched on gave way.

After what seemed to me ages but in fact was no more than a couple of minutes, the boar moved on deeper into the wood and, to my considerable relief out of sight. Even then I remained where I was until I was completely sure he had gone before climbing down onto the ground and out of the wood. I had broken my own rule, a rule I had encouraged others to follow –

if you come face to face with any boar, male or female then back off – never infringe on the animal's space. The scent of the boar alone should have been my signal to withdraw from the area. He would not have felt threatened, and the confrontation would have been avoided. Simple. This would not be the only time that I was to have anxious moments whilst searching for sign of boar but this one instance certainly brought home the speed with which these animals can move – from a standing start to warp speed in the blink of an eye.

Pigs give very little sign that they are upset and intend to do something about it. A dog for example will show his teeth and growl to let you know that he is upset. A bull will paw the ground and snort at you. A ram or goat will back off a few paces before they charge. Boar do none of these things, no warning at all, they just charge! So it's very simple, if you value your well-being its certainly best not to try to get too close. This becomes doubly important if there is the remote possibility of piglets in the area.

Dog walkers should take particular care not to let their dogs out of sight when in areas known to hold boar. Ignore this advice at your peril. On one occasion a woman and her companion were forced to climb a stock fence to get away from a sow and her piglets after the three dogs they were walking, off-lead, wandered into bracken in search of rabbits only to return a few minutes later as the hunted rather than the hunters. Once the perceived threat was over the sow returned to the undergrowth and no harm was done. Understandably, the dog walkers chose to find another way home.

Respect for the countryside

Some folks have very little regard for wildlife and indeed the countryside as a whole. They turn up at a parking spot in a wood or forest, open the car and let the dogs run free. One particular lady on being advised of sows and piglets in the woodland nature reserve retorted belligerently that the woods were her and her dogs' recreation area and marched off defiantly. Her dogs, all seven of them, continued to run off-lead. I cannot understand the mentality of such people. The very fact that she enjoyed walking her dogs in this area was due entirely to the work of the wildlife trust in maintaining the woodland for the benefit of the wildlife. Without their efforts the wood would soon be overrun and frequented by people on mountain bikes, or worse still motor bikes. The long term damage caused by such attitudes to wild life is significant such as birds deserting their nests, deer with fawns at foot being driven from their secure lay up areas and into potentially dangerous human environments and more.

Following my first film of free living wild boar in the south east, I was determined to repeat the exercise the following spring as soon as time and the lighter evenings allowed. Sometime toward the end of February I started to feed the same site at which I had been successful the year before, only at weekends for the first few weeks. As soon as the evenings were light enough, I began feeding mid-week as well. Once the clocks changed at the end of March, I was able to feed every night and this soon paid dividends as the boar began to feed every night and by the end of April I was able to get film of boar on feed and what's more the film was in daylight. The lessons I had learnt the year before standing me in good stead.

Oops!

Throughout that first winter the man from "M" had been busy. He had managed to trap eight boar and fit them with radio collars allowing him to follow the animals with the aid of a mobile receiver. M got some early results from this exercise and was only too pleased to tell me about it. He had established from the tracking that the boar, after foraging, returned to the same spot in the wood each night over a two-week period. However he was puzzled by the recent data. It seemed the boar were no longer laying up where they had previously. They seemed to be scattered over a large area, and this was most unusual. They were not remaining together and were not moving around. He asked me to join him in a daylight search to locate them. Using the hand-held receiver we homed in on the first signal. It didn't take long to discover why the signal we were tracking was not moving. It was no longer attached to the boar but instead lay in a hollow under a redwood tree! The look on the face of the man from the ministry was something I will treasure for the rest of my days! We later found all the collars in the same useless state. Unfortunately these collars were designed for deer. The shape of a boar from shoulder to snout is totally different to that of the red deer and within a short while they simply slipped off. Embarrassing certainly, but there had been a plus to all this. When the boar were captured for the tracking device to be fitted, they were also ear-tagged. The tags were identical to those used by farmers to mark their animals, each carrying a unique number. The tag allowed the boar to be recognised from a distance through a pair of binoculars. Males were tagged in the right and females in the left. All the animals tagged were yearlings born the previous spring. It made sense to only trap the yearlings and not the adults. Older animals are less inclined to follow their stomachs and are far more cautious. Stepping into a man-made device such as a trap would be against all their instincts.

So it was back to the drawing board as far as the tracking devices were concerned.

A bit of a fuss

These tagged boar caused a bit of a stir within the local farming community. There was a good level of mistrust that boar were being deliberately released and that the ministry were somehow involved. Of course they were implicated but it was difficult to convince those with the suspicions that there was a perfectly innocent reason for the tagging.

Whatever the case, ministry tagging certainly made life easier for me. I could, at a safe distance, identify the boar that were coming (and those who were not) to my feeding site. The ear tags were a fluorescent yellow and displayed like a beacon, especially at night with a spot light. Sadly this "here I am badge" proved the downfall for many of these animals. It was a field day for the poachers. Locate the tag, aim and fire at the shadow just to the left or right of it, and your boar was in the pot.

Before long the boar feeding at my site became used to my visits. They would stand back in the bushes out of sight and watch as the food went down. Sometimes the boar were on the feed site before I had walked the 160 yards back to the car. The yearlings were soon joined by an adult female attending each night. At one stage I had four adults and seven yearlings on feed at the same time. Their confidence grew to a point where they were happy to feed within 30 yards of the car. They held no fear of the car but if I stepped out they were gone and would not return until after dark.

As soon as I had established this routine, I notified the Forestry Commission of the boar in this location and advised them that I was feeding in order to film for personal and ministry use. Two nights later I arrived on site and became instantly aware that something was not right. Brambles had been disturbed and closer inspection revealed blood on the track leading to the site. There were tyre tracks leading into the wood finishing by the patch of blood. Persons unknown had taken advantage of this feeding site to shoot one or possibly two boar. Whoever the culprit was would have needed a Forestry Commission key because the gates were locked and were kept that way unless there was work going on in the wood. Even then the gates were locked at night. I wanted to talk this over with the man from the ministry, but he was somewhere in East Anglia on regular duties counting swans or some such thing. He was spending more time away from the boar survey than with it. A sure indicator as far as I was concerned that the ministry was losing interest in wild boar.

First losses by poachers

After the poaching incident, and, as it turned out, the loss of two boar, I stopped feeding altogether at that location. I was not prepared to put the boar at risk in this way for the sake of my studies. I needed to find another site away from the road, a site that could not be easily reached. I enlisted the help of the man from the ministry. We quickly found a suitable spot well away from prying eyes. For added security, Mr "M," using his ministry land rover took the feed to the site during the daytime. This enabled me to walk to the site in the evenings, lightly loaded. Given the site was a mile and a half from the nearest road, I was most grateful for this arrangement. He also benefitted by getting an update on everything that happened while he was away on other duties and of course my latest video footage.

After six months the ministry for reasons best known to itself decided that a further update was needed and our scientist, the man from "M" was asked to write a report on his latest findings. An internal report that is, not intended for public consumption, perhaps to avoid undue alarm. This report prompted the ministry to commission a further study. One might logically expect that the work would be offered to the person who had done all the ground work thus far. He, after all was the only person with the local knowledge to effectively undertake the task. But then whoever said that the ministry had to behave logically. It decided in its wisdom to offer the opportunity to bid for the commission to several others including the author of the initial report. M therefore had to apply for his own job. As it turned out, following presentations, he got the commission. It was a full six months before he got back fully into the swing of things. The ministry, may be short of common sense but they certainly have plenty of time on their hands. Whilst this was going on, I just got more and more hooked on observing the lives and antics of wild boar.

The lessons learned by the man from "M" in his first trapping and tracking experiences had proved invaluable. He had now built some new traps designed specifically for boar, much larger than the borrowed traps used the year before. The radio tracking device was now attached to the ear tag and there they would stay. Also the tags were no longer fluorescent yellow but black. An excellent idea to afford the boar some added security.

Unfortunately black ink had been used to cover the fluorescent yellow. It soon wore off making the tagged boar vulnerable once again. The five animals trapped and tagged again became the target of every person with a gun, poacher or not. These people were intent on foiling the efforts of the man from the ministry. He was, after all, intent on eradicating the boar population and thereby depriving them of what had become a nice little income, or so they thought. For some reason there is an inherent dislike by country folk of ministry employees no matter who they are. "Wouldn't trust em as far as I could throw my tractor" seemed to sum up the general feeling.

Of the five boar caught and tagged, two were killed within a fortnight, and one more a few weeks after that. One young male and one young female were still tagged and we followed their wanderings with the tracking equipment installed in the vehicle – much easier than trudging through the undergrowth with a hand held tracking receiver. All that was needed was to drive to a suitable high point where it was possible to search over a range of several kilometres. Locating a signal in this way was much easier, as was tracking the boar's route each night as it went in search of food. One thing that was most important was the need to retract the telescopic aerial which extended to 20 feet, before moving from one location to another, a fact that was forgotten by the man from "M" on one occasion resulting in an embarrassing call to head office, and a decidedly limp aerial.

By the end of March the signal from the female was from the same location, every time we tried to locate her. The transmitter was designed to operate for a year or so without the need to recapture the animal and replace the battery. If the animal was unfortunately dead we would still get a signal. This went on for about two weeks and we began to fear the worst. Then to our relief the signal began to move again; a short distance at first but further each day though always remaining in the same patch of woodland. Whereas before she would follow the male for several kilometres each night in search of food, now she stayed in the lay up wood all the time. After a week or so she moved out of this area and into another piece of woodland close-by returning to her laying up spot again before dawn. We pinpointed on our map where she had left the wood. We hid out at this location to try to catch a glimpse of her if she crossed the road again into the next wood.

Curious to see why the female was behaving in this way, we tracked her signal from our hideout. Her signal was fluctuating, one minute loud and clear then hardly any signal at all and then it would become clear again. Did we have a faulty transmitter? I had time to think about this and then it struck me. Was the reason for the fluctuating signal that the sow was turning her head from one side to the other? It made sense but why? Was she injured or sick or what? Or could she perhaps have piglets? Not possible. She was only tagged just over two months ago and we would have noticed something like that. Besides the drugs used to anaesthetise the sow whilst blood and tissue samples were taken would surely have caused her to abort. The signal came closer and her behaviour as reflected by the signal, to my mind was consistent with a mother's actions. I pictured her moving through the undergrowth constantly turning round to check that her piglets were following. She got to the edge of the wood and stood just out of sight for several minutes before emerging into the open. She paused and stood listening and scenting the air. Satisfied that all was well she returned to the edge of the wood gave a soft grunt and crossed the track, followed by three piglets! These were the first piglets that I had seen. What a wonderful sight. The mystery of the fading signals was now explained.

Within a few weeks of these piglets' sighting, the sow became another victim of the local stalkers. What became of her piglets is uncertain. Piglets become self sufficient after about eight to ten weeks so they may have made it. As they were my first piglet sighting I would like to think so. There was a report of a piglet caught in a fox snare a few days after the sow was killed, but whether this was one of the three I will never know. Without the sow's guidance it would not have realised the danger presented by the strange scent that would have been present on the snare.

This type of snare is a real danger to inquisitive piglets and there have been several occasions where piglets have been caught in this way. Snares are a perfectly legal means of pest control. The problem with them is that they do not discriminate and once an animal is caught there is little chance of escape. The type of snare used by the poachers for boar and deer on the other hand are totally illegal. These snares are much heavier than the ones used for foxes. They are made from steel-wire rope, the sort of cable used for towing a car. I and like-minded folks will destroy any such devices when we find them in woodland.

So how had this youngster managed to produce a litter of piglets when she herself was only just over a year old? It was commonly supposed that wild boar had to reach 18 months of age to be mature enough to breed successfully. This we now know is not the case. Age has very little to do with it. The governing factors to successful mating are size and food availability.

First litter sows

The sow had produced three piglets that we knew of. She may have produced more and lost them in one way or other. First litter sows are not as experienced as second or third litter animals and are therefore likely to lose piglets, for example accidentally laying on the babies in the nest. So how had she managed to produce these piglets at her young age? The previous autumn had been a good one with reasonable weather and a bumper crop of fruits of the forest. Acorns and chestnuts were plentiful and carpeted the ground, crunching under foot as you walked through the woods. The wild crab apple trees were loaded with fruit, branches straining to breaking point. Hazelnuts adorned every tree and squirrels were working overtime storing as many as they could before they were eaten by something else. These were perfect conditions for the boar to gorge themselves. An adult boar needs about a kilo of protein-rich food a day in order to maintain condition. Any more and the boar gains weight.

Therefore the young females, born the previous spring had plenty of food available to them and were able to gain enough weight to bring them into breeding condition.

A study group in France determined that 45kg is the minimum weight required for sows to breed successfully. Below this sows would not be mature enough to breed. If one female from the previous year's youngsters had managed to breed how many more had done the same? Again unanswerable at that time. Some idea of the piglet numbers born the previous spring would be gleaned from assessing how many animals were in the woods running up to the rut in the coming Autumn.

Radio tagging of boar in this way was useful in as much as it gave an idea of the sort of area covered each night by the various animals. The sounders rarely travel more than a couple of miles from their home range in search of food nearly always returning to the same wood after their night's wanderings.

Having located a new feeding site, I was able to get more footage during the summer months. The boar are nearly always short of food during the hottest months of the year and my supplementary food was always well received. I did not want them to become dependent on my feed and took care to just supply enough to keep them occupied for a short while to allow me to film. I got some very good footage of boar in their summer coat. However, these feed visits were confined to youngsters about six to seven months old and born that year. At about this age they begin to lose their stripes and start to take on a more uniform colour usually with a very faint reddish tinge. This transition stage from six to twelve months of age is known on the continent as "being in the red" and is quite noticeable from a distance but less so close up. I still had not seen the piglets or adult sows known to be in the area. They were probably visiting the site, which was incidentally in an open area that I could observe from a distance, after dark, clearing up any feed left behind by the younger animals.

By the end of the summer a dominant male had also moved into the area. His scent shouted out his presence. A boar in rut has a unique smell, sweet sickly and intense, it hangs in the air like a cloud; a once experienced never forgotten odour. The dominant male breeding wild boar is a nomad and will only stay over in a particular area for one reason – to mate with as many females as he can before another male moves him on. Being nomadic he does not hold territory and therefore has no reason to mark his domain in the way other animals do. The boar will only stay with the sows for as long as there is a chance to mate. Once that chance has passed he will move on to another area in search of more sows. Scent is an important part of the rut. The male produces a pheromone from a gland in the roof of his mouth which induces the female to stand and allow the boar to mate. This of course only happens if the female is in season and ready to mate.

I should point out that this scent is not available over the counter at Boots or any other pharmacy that I could find!

Once a sow becomes receptive the boar will keep pushing her about with his snout until she is ready to mate which she indicates by standing rigid with her ears back along her neck. This is where the gland in the boars mouth comes into play. By constantly exhaling in the sows face, the scent has a stupefying effect on the sow and she stands as if in a trance. Once she has reached this state the boar can walk away from her and she will continue to stand and wait for him to mount her. Usually he will not move far from his conquest and, once he is sure that there are no rivals about to disturb him, mating will take place. It is at this stage that the male boar is at his most dangerous, he will attack anything that moves, human or otherwise, and mean it. Having said this boar do not need any excuse to fight it just comes naturally.

Unlike most animals where the mating act is a brief affair, the boar take their time and the act can take as long as 20 minutes. The boar will stay with the sow after mating to ensure that no other male has access to her and he will continue to mate with her as long as she remains receptive, usually for about 24 to 36 hours. After this time he will move on and start the process all over again with another sow. If the pairing is successful the sow will produce piglets in three months three weeks and three days, if not she will come into season again in three weeks' time.

Food availability and dominance

Not all the sows in a sounder will mate and produce piglets every year. A typical sounder of, say, five sows in a good year when food is plentiful may all have piglets. The dominant sow will have the largest number of offspring and the lowest female in order of dominance will have the least. Twelve to fourteen piglets between them is not unusual but by no means certain. In a bad year when food is scarce, there may be only two of the five who produce any piglets with as few as three or four offspring for the whole group. In these years the sows who do not have piglets of their own will act as baby sitters to the piglets that are born. Taken together with the piglets or yearlings as they would be from the year before and a herd of 20 to 30 animals is not uncommon.

Some sows go through their entire life which can be as long as 10 or 12 years, having only two or three litters of piglets, the number of litters determined by their position in the herd. Dominance plays a vital part in the life of a wild boar. Observations have shown that sows that have been mated successfully have not come into season again after mating and do not always produce a litter that year. It is these sows who will act as minders to the offspring of their superiors for that season.

Another sure sign of the presence of a dominant male in the area for the rut was the larger foot prints found following the tracks left by the sounder as it went about its nightly foraging. It was also the time in late September and early October running up to the rut that reports of road traffic accidents began to occur. It was nearly always young males that were involved. The young males were being driven out from the sounder by the alpha (dominant) male as he moved into the area for the rut. The alpha male will not tolerate another male around his females and will defend them from all-comers until he becomes old or weak and is in turn ousted by a younger, bigger, stronger animal. Most of these encounters result in no contact between the males at all, it being enough for the larger of the two to show his size in profile.

Males have also been observed parallel walking whilst assessing each other's strength. A ritual normally associated with red deer stags. Boar have a row of bristles along their spine which can be raised rather like a porcupine's quills which can add as much as six or seven inches in height to the appearance of the boar and this along with flashing tusks of the larger animal is enough to persuade the would-be challenger to leave. Two equally matched males, however, have been known to fight until one is so badly injured it is unable to continue. The fighting is fierce and can occasionally result in a fatality. The victor lays claim to the females in the sounder and thereby father's the next generation.

Boar tusks

Boar tusks which are in fact elongated canines are for defence or display only. They serve no other purpose. Both male and female have tusks but only the males grow to the sort of length that we see in the trophy heads on the walls of museums and country houses. The male tusks grow throughout their lives and can reach five or six inches long with a further eight inches set in the lower jaw making a total of 12 to 14 inches in all. The upper jaw tusks are not as long as those in the bottom jaw and are used to sharpen, to razor-sharp, the inside edge of the lower tusks. Both sets of tusks curl upwards. In the females the tusks are used for defence or intimidation and are only slightly longer than the rest of their teeth.

The tusks start to grow in the piglets as soon as they are born. Because of the way the tusks grow in the males, i.e. outwards and upwards, means that holding on to a live animal such as a lamb would be almost impossible. They do have, however, very strong jaws that are capable of effortlessly grinding up animal bones.

Above: Sounder of wild boar on feed site in East Sussex, sounder contained four lactating sows and five yearling females without piglets. *Below:* Farmed wild boar on a boar farm at Tenterden in Kent.

Above: A typical example of a European wild boar sow. *Below:* The first photograph of free living wild boar taken in the south east.

Above: Fruits of the forest, Beach Mast, a favourite food of the boar.
Below: An abundance of acorns, the preferred food of the wild boar.

Above: This sort of damage to stock fencing gets the boar a bad reputation. *Below:* More fence damage. This time to a supposedly rabbit-proof fence.

Above: Wild boar tusk marks on a silver birch sapling. *Below:* Stockholm Tar on a mature western hemlock in Beckley Forest, East Sussex. The boar is attracted to the smell of the tar as an insect repellent.

Above: A contented group of wild boar piglets on a feeding site in East Sussex. Below: This group of piglets wait patiently in line for the all-clear signal before venturing out of the cover to feed.

Above: Wild boar sow after a visit to the man-made rubbing tree. The black marks are Stockholm Tar. *Below:* Alpha male and his intended. The boar stands about four feet high at the shoulder and is approximately seven feet long.

Above: Wild boar yearlings during late summer clearly showing coat colour change during the warmer months. *Below:* Mixed group of boar searching for food on a clearing ride.

Above: Family group of wild boar sows and their piglets, the light-coloured animal at top left is a yearling female with no piglets and acts as a lookout. *Below:* Mixed group of pregnant sows and empty yearlings by a wallow. A rubbing tree can be seen top left of picture.

Above: An abandoned farrowing nest on the edge of a fir plantation, East Sussex. *Below:* At first glance just a pile of vegetation. Closer inspection reveals a day nest used by wild boar sows to suckle their young for the first few days after leaving the farrowing nest.

.

Chapter Three

The Rut

THERE ARE several factors that trigger the rut, the first is the availability of food. In years when food, for example acorns and chestnuts etc, are plentiful the sows will put on weight and condition quickly and this brings them into breeding condition sooner than in a year when food is scarce. The second factor is the shortening daylight hours and the drop in temperature which comes with late autumn. There is a marked change in behaviour of the males at this time of the year as autumn approaches. What until now had been friendly sparring on their part now becomes more aggressive as they seek to establish their position in the herd. As the testosterone levels rise in the males so does the aggression until the dominance or otherwise is settled. The losers will move on and form bachelor groups until the following spring when they will rejoin the group. The sows in the mean time just get on with their own dominance battles. The rut, in a good year, when food is plentiful will get under way by the second week in October, the same as on the continent. The difference is that on the continent the rut will last about five or six weeks with the farrowing season complete by the end of March whereas here in the south east of England it is not unusual for the boar to still be running with the sows in late

April. This means that not only do we have an extended rut we also have an extended farrowing season with piglets being born from late February through to July.

Importance of dominance

The sows come into season in order of seniority, the dominant sow first, followed by the next in line and so on. The females are able to breed at ten months old provided they have access to the right food and in the right quantity. Studies on the continent suggest that a live weight of 45kg is the point at which the females become receptive to the boar. So the position of a female in the herd is of vital importance; the time period between the sows being mated determines the time differences between farrowing and therefore the dominant sow's piglets will be born as much as a week before the next sow in line. Her piglets will be that much older than the rest of the herd and so always dominant over the other piglets in the group.

A sounder is usually made up of a sow and her female offspring, in some cases comprising three or four generations, i.e. her daughters, granddaughters, great granddaughters. It might also include other close relations such as her sisters and their previous female offspring. The gestation period for the wild boar is the same as domestic pigs, three months three weeks three days give or take a few hours. The sows are in season for only 24 to 36 hours and once mated the boar will turn his attention to the next in line, guarding her until she too is mated. Sometimes he will go as far as to drive other dominant, already-mated sows away from food in order to bring the sow he is courting in to season sooner, particularly if the female is a youngster. I witnessed this act one evening. I was at a feed site with some friends when a group of boar turned up, five females and one large male, among them a female a bit smaller than the rest. From their shape and demeanour, the others were clearly much older and pregnant. The boar continually flashing his tusks, kept these sows away from the feed allowing his intended a full and uninterrupted dinner. When the young female was fully fed he left the site with the youngster finally allowing the pregnant sows to feed. This staggered mating is the reason for the different sized piglet groups seen around the end of August. Wild boars come into season and produce just the one litter per year.

Studies of boar during the rut undertaken in France have shown that a dominant boar may not feed at all whilst he is holding sows, instead spending all his time protecting his harem from the attentions of other would-be suitors. One boar under surveillance was seen not to eat for a full six weeks by which time he had lost almost half his body weight. The effect of this loss of weight meant that he was no longer strong enough to defend his sows from stronger competitors and lost his herd to a rival. Although timing is plainly a factor, generally, as is the way with the natural world, the strongest and fittest prevail and thereby sustain a strong healthy population. The alpha male plays no part in the rearing of the piglets. Having assured himself all his females are pregnant he will spend the rest of the year in isolation as far away from the sows and piglets as he can. His focus returns to food and restoring strength and weight to ready himself for the run up to the next rut.

Sows feed throughout the rut as they have no need to fight off other females for the attentions of the boar. The sow's position in the group's pecking order ensure that her turn will come soon enough. Sows are loosely territorial, remaining in one area of the countryside moving on only when harassed by hunters or packs of dogs and of course when food gets scarce. One thing boar enjoy more than anything is peace and quiet; confrontation is not for them. Locations disturbed on a regular basis by dogs, the local gamekeeper or woodsman will not hold boar for long but this is not to say that they will not visit these forest or woodland areas from time to time in search of food.

Farrowing

Sows continue to feed right up until a few hours before they give birth at which time they will leave the sounder and find themselves an isolated spot in which to build their farrowing nest. The nest bed is constructed of grass, straw or bracken which has been chewed into short pieces to make it safe for the new arrivals. This is then deposited in a shallow depression which has been excavated by the sow in readiness. The greatest danger to newly born piglets is getting laid on by the sow as they try to move around the nest to find a nipple to feed from, an instinctive act almost as soon as they are born. The entire nest once built, is covered with a heap of whatever vegetation is available. The sow hides herself under this pile whilst she gives birth and remains in the nest until the piglets are strong enough to follow her in search of food. She does not produce milk until an hour or two before she gives birth when milk can sometimes be seen dripping from the teats. The piglets, having found a teat, will feed from that teat and no other throughout the time it is suckling. The sows produce milk in all teats and once the piglets get used to their respective teats the nipples that are not in use will be dried-off within a few days and milk will only be available to the selected teats. This ensures that the sow only has to produce enough milk to supply the needs of her own offspring. It is in part the reason why a wild boar sow will not suckle another sow's piglets. In addition, her basic instinct is to improve her standing and that of her piglets in the sounder. To feed another's piglets would undermine this fundamental objective.

Should the sow become unable to feed her piglets perhaps due to sickness or injury or she is killed by poachers, her piglets, if not old enough to fend for themselves, will die. If this happens then the next litter of piglets in order of seniority will move up a notch in the pecking order.

When the piglets are 10 to 14 days old, they are strong enough to leave the nest and follow the sow. She will introduce the piglets to their relatives. The sows take particular care to ensure there are no alpha males in the area before venturing out from the security of the nest. An alpha male coming across the piglets would almost certainly kill them. This said, he would do the same if he came upon the nest. If on the other hand he is the father of those piglets he will defend them in the same way the sows will. This is also true of females within the sounder who also would kill the piglets if they got the chance but only when the sow and her piglets are at their most vulnerable, i.e. in the nest. This fact alone is one of the reasons the sows seek an isolated location in which to give birth, even shunning their own family members.

Devoted mothers

Sows are particularly devoted mothers and will not put their piglets at risk. If a sow has the slightest doubt about the safety of a feeding site, she will move her offspring in search of another site. On one occasion, I inadvertently disturbed a group of four sows and 13 piglets that I had been trying to get a look at for several evenings. They had been arriving at nightfall so I had had little success with filming. This evening they had arrived two hours ahead of their usual schedule for reasons unknown. They took off at the sound of my approach. After that fright I never saw them again on that site. However, some eight weeks later I received a phone call from a local retired gamekeeper informing me that a group of animals matching this description had been seen regularly feeding in broad daylight in a field of clover. They had been there for several weeks. This came as quite a surprise. My understanding was that wild boar were pretty much nocturnal especially when they had piglets at foot, and were not expected to be found out in the open during daylight hours.

The dominant sow in a sounder normally decides where and when the sounder will feed or wallow and will lead the group, followed by the piglets with the rest of the adults bringing up the rear. At the sound of a grunted warning from one of the sows, the piglets will instantaneously drop into whatever cover they may be standing in. Their stripes provide excellent camouflage making it almost impossible to see them in the gloom of the forest. Unless seen taking cover, you would most certainly not know they were there. This sort of response from the piglets continues for two to three weeks after they leave the safety of the nest but as both their confidence and bodies grow, the response becomes less dramatic. Their seemingly insatiable appetite soon gets the better of them and they are back to foraging for morsels – however small or unappetising they might be.

Testing technology

The piglets' curiosity leads them to investigate everything they come across. Everything is tested to see if it is edible including, on one occasion to my personal cost, a memory card containing a considerable number of photos taken over a week or more of filming. I realised I had lost it on reaching home one evening. Too late to return that night, I went back to the hide at the feed site the following evening. It wasn't in the hide and extending the search became like looking for the proverbial needle in a haystack. I gave up and forgot about it. About a week later, I was scattering the feed at the same site and there on the ground in the middle of the feed area was the missing device. It was still recognisable though bent slightly out of shape and with several pin holes in it where the piglets had chewed it. After straightening, it still fitted the camera but the images were no longer recognisable. The piglets had decided it had a better use as a teething ring.

Nomadic boar

The males will travel a considerable distance in a night in search of sows. One night a boar was seen crossing the road behind a group of sows between Rye and Peasmarsh in east Sussex. It was almost hit by a car and that same boar which had an unmistakable distinctive mark to his face was involved in a serious road traffic accident between Battle and Ninfield, some fifteen miles away the following night. There was serious damage both to the vehicle and the boar which struggled away from the scene. It was found a few days later by a dog walker, having succumbed to his injuries. That this was the same animal is not in doubt, the fact that he was of a lighter colouration than most and the distinctive scar to his face the give away.

The male's nomadic lifestyle unfortunately makes him an easier target for the poachers and also explains why we very often find tracks of a single boar in the most unlikely of places such as along the edge of a field and many miles away from the nearest patch of woodland. This also explains why, during the first few years of freedom, it was nearly always males that were being killed on the road or by hunters. For the most part the males used the same tracks each night. This made it very easy for the poachers to lay down their traps and snares in thick patches of forest to catch the unsuspecting boar as they trod their regular routes. That this practice was illegal did not deter the poachers. There only concern was to get out early in the morning to inspect their snares before the rest of us well aware that if they didn't that would be the last they would see of their dastardly hardware. The only sign that boar had been caught in this way would be an area of flattened undergrowth caused by the boar or, in some cases deer, as they struggled in vain to break free.

Alerts about such poacher traps being deployed in an area were generally circulated via the local game dealers. Such alerts would most often result in the immediate mobilisation of local estates' staff to seek and destroy the snares. The Forestry Commission, the largest managers of woodland in the country, were always finding such snares and on just one occasion I was aware of 15 such snares recovered and held at their area depot near Goudhurst in Kent.

Desperate measures
One estate owned by Sir Paul McCartney was visited by poachers more than most (and still is). Sir Paul's love of animals led people to believe that the estate was a haven for boar and deer, indeed at one time the estate was accused of deliberately releasing wild boar into the countryside. Complete rubbish

of course. Whilst the deer may be plentiful, the estate spent hundreds of thousands of pounds on fences in an attempt to ensure that the boar did not find a sanctuary on the estate. However, these measures proved to be no match for the sheer determination of wild boar. As a result the fences had to be further strengthened to prevent the boar from both jumping over and digging under. These reinforced fences have proved successful in keeping down the boar numbers getting onto the estate but has resulted in other animals also being kept out. The wire size causes problems for rabbits, and the 5.5 feet high fences are also a challenge for deer. This leads to occasional accidents. Deer have been found hung up in the fence where they have tried to jump from field to woodland or vice versa. Some of these hang ups if found soon enough result in little harm to the deer and they bound away shaken but otherwise unhurt. In some instances the animal is dead before it is found and sadly most of these fatalities are youngsters who have tried to follow their mothers over the fence with tragic results. Wildlife does not understand that the fence that has gone up across their traditional track through the forest is there to stop them doing what they and their ancestors have done for hundreds of years. Badgers show no intention of giving up their rights to roam free and they have in places dug under this fence which is buried up to two feet in the ground in order to get to their feeding areas. There are also a few places where a pair of wire cutters have been used to aid the passage of some of the smaller mammals. The tenacity and determination of wildlife never ceases to amaze me. They seem always to find a way to work around the obstacles we put in their way.

Unpredictability

Things are constantly changing and no two years are ever the same. Just when you think you've got it all worked out, the boar do something different and you have to rethink your understanding of them. A friend said one day that the only thing predictable about the wild boar is its unpredictability.

For instance, it will for no apparent reason, suddenly disappear from an area that looked to have everything they could possibly want, sometimes for weeks at a time, only to return quite out of the blue, but then that's what makes life interesting, isn't it?

It is generally accepted that wild boar have been extinct in this country since around 1680, with the last boar being killed in the New Forest or Aberdeenshire depending on what you read and who you believe. There is a minority school of thought particularly among the fanatical bunny huggers that the boar did not die out at all but that they have simply been hiding. I think not; if an animal as big and prolific as the wild boar had been roaming the countryside for the last 350 years, I think we would have noticed. Even us country yokels would have noticed something like that – after filling the freezer first of course.

There are wild boar or their close relatives across most of the world including Wart Hogs, Peccaries, Jabalina, Red River Hogs. The wild boar roaming free in England are, for the most part, European in origin of which there are two types, the western European, i.e. French and the low countries, and eastern European, i.e. Russian. Interestingly, the wild boar on the Kent and Sussex border are the western European variety and those in the east of the county are eastern European. This suggests two escapes from two quite separate herds but it will only be a matter of time before the two combine. Both species look very similar with the only noticeable difference being colour and size. The Russian or eastern European are darker and slightly heavier than their western cousins. There is also a mix of other types of domestic blood in certain areas of the country including Tamworth, Iron Age Pig, Black Berkshire, etc. When comparing the photographs and film of boar from across the country the difference in parentage is quite noticeable especially in those animals deliberately released from boar farms in the west of England who all show a definite lean towards the old English breeds, in particular iron age pigs, the closest relatives to the true wild boar.

Wild boar hunting

The domestic blood came about as a result of cross breeding domestic animals with wild boar sows to try to reduce aggression and increase the number of piglets per litter. This was after all a commercial enterprise and the more piglets per sow the more profit at the end of the year. The Russian or Black Russian as it is also known is famed for its size and aggression throughout the world and was introduced into North America and Canada for hunting purposes and is now widespread throughout North America and looked upon as a worthy adversary. It receives a great deal of respect amongst hunters throughout the U.S. and indeed the rest of the world. Hunters are prepared to pay large sums of money for the chance to bag a Black Russian.

The Celtic tribes had so much respect for the strength and aggression of the wild boar that when a boy killed his first boar he was deemed to have become a man. With no rifles or shot guns then mind, just a flint knife or spear and a heavy dose of courage, his elevation to manhood would have been fully justified. The boar also featured on the war banners of the tribes. The symbol of a boar also appears on several coats of arms to this day particularly in Germany.

Wild boar hunting is a popular and expensive business throughout most of the world. Following the break up of the Soviet Union the emerging countries of the former eastern block are now the hot spots as far as boar hunting is concerned with Hungary and Croatia, along with Germany and Russia, the most sought after destinations for hunters who wish to obtain a medal winning trophy for the study wall.

Strict regulations currently govern the hunting of wild boar in Europe and some states in America and Canada. However, some US states and indeed many other countries have very few regulations at all, Australia and New Zealand with their large populations of feral hogs or Captain Cookers, as they are more popularly known, are considered a pest and can be shot or killed by any means available which includes poison baits. However, these feral hogs are not true wild boar but the result of domestic stock gone wild, some as the result of escapes and others as the result of failed farming activities with the pigs abandoned to fend for themselves. Boar hunting in Australia is carried on as you would expect by any means possible including helicopters, quad bikes, horses, four-wheel drive vehicles, with dogs and I am sure many other imaginative ways. There are those who still like to hunt the hogs with dogs in Australia and New Zealand dogs are specially bred for the job.

They pursue the pigs until the animal has had enough of being chased and stands at bay, daring the dogs to come in close and fight. The dogs are, in most cases, trained to stay just out of reach of the pigs' fearsome tusks until the owner arrives on the scene to dispatch the boar, usually with a shot from a gun. This is not always the case. There remain a hardy few who prefer to dispatch the animal by hand, with a knife. Perhaps it should be 'mad dogs, Australians and New Zealanders'!

Europe on the other hand generally looks on the wild boar as an asset to be managed. Money generated by boar hunting throughout Europe runs into many millions of Euros each year drawing hunters from all over the world. In some districts in France, farms used to cross wild boar with domestic sows for the local restaurant trade. Surplus stock was released into the forest to supplement the wild stock so as to give the visiting hunters a greater variety of targets where numbers were important rather than quality. This had the effect, in some areas, of diluting the wild boar blood line to such an extent that the boar were no longer pure boar but a cross breed. This is the reason for some of the multi-coloured animals that can be seen in France today. This domestic blood would soon be bred out over the years, and the true wild boar characteristics would show through and in most cases this has proved to be the case, although just occasionally the odd coloured pig shows up.

Eastern European countries however with their stricter regulations have managed to maintain a more or less true blood line and produce some of the best trophy heads in the world. Close seasons are imposed to protect sows and piglets in order to maintain a good head of animals for what is a very valuable asset both to the local population who benefit from the added income generated by the hunters and their followers and to the country's wider economy. With boar hunting as popular as it is, it has been found necessary to maintain strict control as to the numbers killed each year, and every animal killed is meticulously recorded and tagged with a tamper proof tag so as to allow the carcase to be traced from forest to table. The carcase is also examined and tested to make sure it is fit for human consumption and free from any of the diseases that all members of the pig family are susceptible to. This has a two-fold benefit, first to be sure that the carcase is fit for human consumption and secondly provide an early warning of any potential disease issues.

This unfortunately currently is not the case in the UK with the animals entering the food chain unregulated and therefore there is no early warning system such as that which is available on the continent. This potentially places the public at risk from unchecked boar carcases entering the food chain through the back door.

Germany is reported to have the largest population of wild boar in Europe with an estimated 2,500 animals living in the suburbs of Berlin alone. In the 70s before the Berlin wall came down there were over 120,000 boar killed by hunters in East and West Germany combined, each year. Compare these numbers with the estimated 2,500 animals in the whole of Britain and perhaps it is not too surprising that the powers that be have such a relaxed attitude toward wild boar. That is of course unless it happens to be your field or crop that is receiving the boar's attention.

UK firearm's regulations

The current regulations concerning the taking of wild boar in the UK are not as simple as most sane thinking people would like, the recommendations are vague and varied from county to county depending on the firearms' officers employed in the area in which the licence is applied for, some insisting on strict control and conditions of use, others being more relaxed in the granting of such variations to the applicants licence, but all recommend a minimum shell calibre of .270 or above. This in itself is a bone of contention among shooting people, some recommend a larger calibre others would be quite happy to use the calibre recommended for the control of red deer, that being .243, arguing that if the weapon is suitable for the control of red deer over a distance of 200 yards or more, then it should be capable in the right hands of controlling wild boar over much shorter distances. The distances that boar are taken at are not likely to be more than 70 yards, where placement of shot is all the more important. If a person applying for the licence in the first place is not capable of a grouping of five shots in a three inch circle at 70 yards then they should not be given a certificate, period. There are some people who are truly amazing shots with a rifle, there was one chap who consistently killed boar with a hornet which is only recommended for foxes and rabbits, and there are those who take boar and deer regularly with a crossbow all of which are illegal and frowned upon by the powers that be, and until the wild boar are recognised for what they are the situation will not change.

They won't survive

The rise in popularity of wild boar farming undoubtedly led to today's free living wild boar. The escapees from farms and private collections were responsible for the first viable breeding groups located in the Kent and Sussex borders. Their appearance elsewhere was a result of deliberate release of whole herds through the misguided actions of well meaning individuals. Boar is now established in viable breeding groups all over the country, as far north as Scotland, into Wales and other parts of Southern England. At first those in authority were convinced that the boar would not survive in the countryside of the twentieth century. Ninety percent of the woods and forests of the seventeenth century that were home to the boar had disappeared, consumed by the insatiable appetite of a growing human population. There was also a need for timber to build ships with which to defend the country and to help build an empire. Where once there were unbroken tracks of trees and forests save an occasional hamlet, there are now towns, cities, motorways and railways which have decimated these havens for not only wild boar, but also all the other woodland animals and birds. The modern boar had not read the script and immediately upon escape or release sought out twentieth century countryside and disappeared into it. Remarkably, or perhaps not so depending on your point of view and familiarity with the beast, they adapted and, in most cases establishing a thriving breeding population.

If the people in charge of the country, MAFF in those early days, in the 1980s and 90s, had listened to and acted on the reports that were coming into their offices, the situation here in the south east as far as the boar were concerned could have been avoided, and the small number of boar that had escaped could, almost certainly have been contained, instead we weren't believed, nor were we listened to, after all people who did not work for the government or have letters after their name could not possibly know what they were talking about, and the whole thing was probably just another "beast of Exmoor" story. I could never understand that if I see something it can't possibly be right, but if a person with letters before or after their name sees the same thing, it is taken as gospel and should not be questioned, that's just life I suppose.

Basic requirements to survive

The basic requirements for boar to succeed are, habitat, water and food. A thick woodland or undergrowth in which to lay up during daylight hours is essential, the thicker and more remote from civilisation the better. Wild boar will take isolation over confrontation any time. This said they are always prepared to stand up for themselves if push comes to shove. There is an old saying in this part of the world "a Sussex man wunt be druv" that is to say he will not be pushed around and this well describes the character of wild boar.

Woodland cover

Young conifer plantations are favourite and ideal laying-up areas with their thick impenetrable growth which gives both shade and cover and also warmth and seclusion for rearing piglets, thus making an ideal nesting site. Thick reed beds are also ideal areas for sows and their piglets to lay up during the summer months in particular. The sows need an isolated area in which to have their piglets away from the rest of the sounder. She will seek an area both thick enough, dry enough and remote enough to suit her needs. This may be an overgrown or dried up pond or reed bed, possibly up to two to three kilometres from their usual haunts. Dog walkers in such areas need to take particular care in the spring not to let their dogs out of sight. Dogs are unaccustomed to encountering a wild animal standing its ground in their presence. A wild boar will do just that and will charge without warning. It takes but a few seconds for an irate sow protecting her piglets to inflict an awful lot of damage to an unsuspecting family pet. Fine if you have good insurance cover to pay the vet's bill, not so good for the poor animal. As well as the physical requirements of the habitat, there is of course the requirement for plentiful foraging areas. Patches of mixed woodland are ideal often comprising oak, ash, chestnut, hornbeam, sycamore, maple etc, all of which produce seeds in one form or another and so are ideally suited for wild boar.

Water whether provided by streams, ponds or ditches is a must. Pigs of all kind need a ready supply of fresh drinking water and boar will leave an otherwise ideal habitat for what at first glance seems a less suitable location in respect of cover and food in order to be near a supply of fresh water. They have another good reason to place such a high priority on the proximity to water; boar do not have sweat glands and need damp soggy ground to wallow in to prevent them from over heating. A boar wallow can be quite a noisy spot. Indeed it can be a rather dangerous spot for the younger animals in the sounder. There is a strict bathing order in the wallow with the most dominant animals taking first wallow whilst the others await their turn. Animals of a similar standing in the group will quite happily lay together in a mud hole or wallow until someone more senior comes along and drives them out. Boar will quite often bury themselves almost completely but ever vigilant, only up to their snouts, eyes and ears. The ears and snout remain on full alert – boar sense of smell and hearing are among the best in the animal world and more than compensates for their poor eyesight.

Some of these communal wallows are extensive and the boar will visit them on a regular basis especially in the heat of high summer and times of drought. Such is the pleasure, a good uninterrupted wallow can come before the prospect of a free meal and they will often turn up at the feeding site with the tell tale signs of having first visited the local wallow.

A short distance from their wallows will be a tree designated as their rubbing tree and easily identified by the amount of mud on their trunks. It is not at all unusual to find a rubbing tree that has been completely ring barked, the bark completely worn away exposing the flesh of the trunk and certain death for the tree. Most of these rubbing trees are conifers whose resin the boar use as an insect and parasite repellent. They use their tusks to gouge away slivers of bark causing the pine resin to flow. The boar vigorously rub themselves against the tree to cover their bodies with the resin; an onlooker would, not unreasonably perceive the boar to be in a state of ecstasy, almost wearing a smile and skipping away from the tree like frolicking spring lambs.

Food and foraging areas

The third requirement is of course food. Wild boar are no different in that respect to any other living thing, they need food to survive. Wild boar are omnivores, indeed they will eat almost anything they come across including dead or dying animals, particularly birds and rabbits. These meals are not confined to the woods and forest either but also include road kills and casualties from shooting parties such as pigeons and pheasants. Body size does not inhibit them at all and they will eat any fallen livestock. It is this behaviour that results in them being, in my view, mistakenly blamed for the killing of lambs from a lambing field. I am not aware of any evidence that substantiates boar as lamb killers. I believe they are entitled to the benefit of doubt unless or until such proof is presented. That they dine on dead lambs is not in dispute. It happens every year to some degree and I regularly come across this in my studies.

What is not generally known is that boar are cannibalistic and will in certain circumstances consume their own dead relatives. Boar that die of old age, injury or disease will be eaten by the rest of the sounder. They will drive off other scavengers such as foxes and badgers who also like to feed on dead animals such as lambs of course. The foxes and badgers do a lot more damage to a flock of sheep than wild boar. Badgers in particular are a hazard that every shepherd is mindful of. The results of a visit by badgers to a lambing field can be quite horrific; badgers have a tendency to attack the udders of the ewes, causing damage so severe that the ewe has to be put down which leaves new born lambs to be found homes – more work for an already hard pressed farmer in lambing season.

Whilst boar will take a meat dish any time the opportunity presents itself, most of its food supply is vegetable in the form of roots, bulbs and young shoots. The majority of a boar's waking hours is spent in search of food. Their snouts are working constantly in what seems a completely aimless and random way as it turns over vast quantities of soil in their search for grubs, insects, roots and shoots.

In times of plenty their food consists mainly of fruits of the forest, for example acorns and chestnuts, wild crab apples and other forest produce like fungi. When acorns and chestnuts are plentiful the boar will eat very little else; the level of toxins they contain do not seem to bother the boar to that extent but I have noticed that if boar are feeding on acorns they also tend to root on old pasture in search of earthworms. They also seek out minerals and trace elements which I understand may counter the high amount of toxins absorbed from the acorns and chestnuts. My thinking is that in years when forest fruits are scarce the rooting on pasture land is less severe over the season. This said earthworms and other soil born grubs play a large part in a wild boar's diet and this is especially so after a drought. The onset of the first heavy rains bring the earthworms to the surface and the boar then descend on the fields in numbers and cause considerable damage in a very short time which tends to upset the land owner.

Boar will also take advantage of agricultural crops from time to time. They love maize and can, given the chance, destroy a field of maize in little or no time. They will target the cobs of corn just before they start to ripen when the grains are soft and juicy. Though maize is a favourite the boar will take any crop that takes their fancy. However, a good stock-proof fence is all that is required to keep the boar at bay and prevent damage to agricultural crops and land. In years of scarcity, boar will seek out the food of other animals such as squirrels who store any excess acorns and chestnuts below ground in disused rabbit burrows, sometimes several kilos of food in one place. Gifted with an acute sense of smell, they have little problem locating such caches and using their strong snouts which make effective digging implements will dig down as deep as 60 centimetres (two foot) to reach the harvested stocks painstakingly gathered by the squirrel to see it through a bad winter.

Some of these diggings are six to eight feet long and can cover several square feet. It has been suggested that boar are in fact looking for salts or trace elements in the same way that other animals do, sometimes travelling several miles for their mineral needs. In the case of boar in the south east I think this unlikely. If this were the case the boar would use the same sites year after year and my observations show this simply does not happen. Close inspection of these excavations almost always show the remains of a cache of acorns and, in some cases, the tell tale signs of a nest of baby rabbits, another delicacy on the boars menu. Such diggings are almost always on the site of a disused rabbit burrow. A live rabbit burrow has too much activity for the squirrels' liking and they will almost always seek out an unoccupied premises to store their winter food supply.

By far the biggest and the most important food source is vegetable matter as mentioned earlier. Shoots, bluebell bulbs, pretty much any plants that have a tuberous, fleshy root system are on the boars' wish list. Silver weed, rose bay, willow herb and bracken are eaten by the wild boar during the plants' dormant period when the root system is at its most nutritious. Silver weed is a favourite followed by rose bay, willow herb and finally bracken. In times of hardship though they will eat whatever they can find. Much favoured and before eating any vegetation would be acorns and chestnuts, in fact any variety of natural fruits of the forest. In some parts of the country wild boar have been introduced to areas of scrub and hill with the sole purpose of clearing bracken. Bracken is one of nature's hooligans as far as plants are concerned. It quickly takes over large areas of hill and scrub and is renowned for being very difficult to get rid of. The smallest piece of root will take the opportunity to regrow and recolonise an area previously and painstakingly cleared. Enter wild boar and it is only a matter of time, provided the boar are not given the opportunity to forage more desirable areas, before their constant rooting get the upper hand and the bracken is brought under control. When deployed in this way they are extremely good gardeners. They must be given occasional opportunity to supplement their fare to counter toxins that build up on a constant diet of bracken roots.

Boar and bluebells

During the hardest of times, bluebell woods will also be visited by boar when their bulbs are at their most nutritious. Not being a first choice food, it is possible to an extent to judge the health of an area of woodland by the time of year the boar start to root for bulbs in the bluebell patches. The sight of the devastation left by the boar after they have rooted through a bluebell wood is always saddening – I don't know anyone who isn't moved at the sight of a sea of bluebells in a sun-dappled woodland. But what looks on the surface to be a disaster is not all bad; the boars' rooting does result in some bulbs being eaten but this carnage also releases a large quantity of seeds of not only bluebells but other plants as well and these readily sew themselves into the freshly turned soil giving credence to the saying "boar is nature's gardener". The downside to this is that if the forest fruits fail two or three years in a row then the bluebell patch is completely ruined and may take several years of boar-free activity to recover. Daffodil woods once plentiful, are now, sadly, in decline. True wild daffodils are now very rare so the attentions of a sounder of wild boar are most unwelcome although once again the rooting of the boar has the beneficial effect of planting last season's fallen seeds and once again, if left alone the daffodil woods will recover with an equally impressive display of blooms the following year. The boar may not in fact be rooting for daffodil bulbs; some researchers believe that the daffodil bulbs are in fact poisonous to the boar. The belief is that they are rooting for grubs and earthworms and the damage to the daffodils is collateral damage and not the objective. That bluebell and wild daffodil woods are situated on light sandy soil may also have a bearing on the boars' rooting behaviour. The damage is no less whatever the reason and the jury is out on this one.

Having said all this the reader might be forgiven for thinking that wild boar set out in packs to hunt down the poor unsuspecting creatures that live in our woods. They do not. True they will eat most things that come their way including ground nesting birds and ground living rodents. However, the chances of boar actually catching a ground nesting bird on the nest are remote. Most self-respecting birds will be safely on the wing long before a boar was upon them but the same cannot be said for any young or eggs found in the nest. Any bird that nests more than four feet off the ground is quite safe from the ground-based boar.

Ground living mammals on the other hand tend to go to ground if threatened which is the only invitation the boar needs to start digging – it's favourite pastime. The boar's foraging activities benefit several species of birds and they will congregate around the freshly rooted patches of soil to take advantage of the insects disturbed by the boar in their search for grubs and roots. Magpies are always ready to take advantage of wild boar and will quite happily hop along with the foraging boar, picking up missed morsels of food sometimes no more than a few inches away from the boar's snout but always far enough to be safe. Magpies can also be seen riding on the boar, pecking out parasites, insects and lumps of loose hair, the latter usually in the Spring when they are nest building. This is clearly a mutually beneficial relationship.

The wild boar's appetite, is unfortunately, also it's weakness. Once a family group of boar find a ready free meal, they will return to the same spot again and again until either the food runs out or they find another source of food. The food may be natural or left by man to draw the boar into an area in which to either observe or shoot them. To tempt boar, so that I can observe them, I generally use a mixture of whole maize and grain, usually barley and or wheat. This is often supplemented with other feed such as poultry pellets and dry dog food past its sell by date and due to be dumped. Decidedly unappetising to you and I but a delightfully smelling and desirable dinner for an ever-hungry boar.

Hic!

Like a lot of people I like to take advantage of nature's bounty in the form of sloes and damsons; sloes for sloe gin and the damsons for my favourite damson brandy. Both of which are excellent tipples for the winter months. Now, the method for making each of these beverages is quite simple; select ripe fruit (this is the most important part), wash and clean thoroughly, remove any damaged or unsound fruit, prick each fruit individually at least three times and place in a suitable container. I prefer the old fashioned sweet jars with the screw tops which allows you to see just how well the tipple is progressing. Fill with fruit to just below the shoulder, you can at this stage add a small amount of sugar. I prefer about half a pound at this stage for each jar. You can always add more later if the liquid is not sweet enough but you can't take it out if you add too much. At this point you can then add the gin, brandy, whiskey or any other spirit that takes your fancy. It should cover the fruit. Stir to dissolve the sugar, screw the lid down tightly and leave to soak for at least four months before bottling. With damsons the liquid can be bottled after three months. The fruit can then be used a second time with whatever other spirit of your choice. A friend of mine once told me that he uses accumulated bottles of poor sherry. He swore that this turns a poor drink into one that is quite acceptable.

When I worked with livestock we would feed apple pulp to cattle and pigs, the pulp being the waste from the cider making process. I reasoned why not put the spent fruit from my gin and brandy making to good use too. I had several pounds of excess fruit so I added it to my usual mix to see just how sensitive the boar were to the scent and the unusual. I reasoned that it would at least be an interesting experiment if nothing else.

The extra fruit together with my normal feed and recording equipment made for quite a load and I was glad when I reached the feed site. I scattered the normal feed, put the fruit down in two separate piles and retired to my perch in the high seat. The boar came in as normal but stopped short of the feed site. They stood scenting the air; quite clearly they did not like the strange smell of the alcohol-soaked fruit. After a short while they retreated the way they had come and disappeared. My experiment appeared to have failed spectacularly.

Now what to do? I had two piles of fruit that I would now have to take away lest the boar desert the site altogether. Why did I have to interfere with a set up that was working so well?

As I pondered this the boar suddenly reappeared this time from a different direction.

Cautiously they came right into the feed site and started to feed as normal simply ignoring the fruit. That is until one young inquisitive male decided to see what this strange pile of food was. He carefully took one mouthful and backed away, presumably testing what must have been a strange taste. The other animals appeared to be interested in his reaction. When he again approached the fruit he was joined by two other animals, one male and one female. They too applied the same test stepping back as the first had done. The female was not impressed and returned to her normal feed, the males though began to gobble up as much as they could; so intently, they began to fight for the lion's share.

After half an hour or so the fruit had almost all disappeared and both males were now looking decidedly unsteady, almost as though they were swaying with the breeze. Not surprising really when you consider the amount of alcohol the two had consumed. My reckoning was that they would have been well over the limit if they had been breath tested.

I was now looking forward to some spectacular footage to show people; drunken wild boar, whatever next? What happened next was the battery failed on my camera! Not run out of charge, I was always careful with that, no it just failed and had to be replaced, Murphy had intervened again.

This fruit soaked in alcohol was nothing new, it had been used for years by the old poachers to take pheasants. The fruit was raisins and was soaked in cider for 48 hours before use. After consuming the raisins the birds became incapable in a very short space of time and could be picked up without any problem or more to the point without any noise.

Seafood sundae

Before I recount another story I should confess that I have a bit of a reputation for practical jokes and sometimes my sense of humour can get the better of me. I had some shrimps in my freezer that had been there for far too long. Short of food for the boar I used the shrimps to bulk out the feed bag to be used in a film shoot for a very important programme, for me anyway. The presenter spotted the shrimps as soon as I opened the bag.

"Are those shrimps?" he asked.

"Yes," I replied.

"The boar love them, it's the strong smell that attracts them, they love anything like that with a strong smell."

This is not quite true, in fact its not true at all, boar are completely indifferent to shrimps and will pass them by if other food is on offer. (Foxes on the other hand love them and would scour the whole feeding site if shrimps were sniffed.) I had clearly kept a very straight face because the presenter waxed lyrics to his TV audience about the craving that boar had for shrimps. I offer my apologies now.

Observing roles and status

When observing boar, I found it best to scatter the food over a large area to give all the members of the sounder the chance to find some food without fear of being driven off by a more senior or dominant member. This made it easier to identify individuals and their seniority. It helps too with counting piglets, which sow is suckling which piglets, and how many piglets each sow has. The number of teats in use shows at a glance how many piglets she is feeding. We can also observe which sows are not feeding piglets and are therefore stand-in baby sitters.

Whilst sows are on feed with piglets at foot there will be a senior member of the sounder on guard duty somewhere in the near vicinity. This duty is shared and other adult females will take turn from time to time. This guard duty does not seem to involve the male members of the sounder. Any males that are feeding with sows and piglets are almost always last year's offspring and will not normally be breeding males. At the slightest hint of danger a short growl from the animal on guard is enough to send the rest of the group scampering for cover. All members of the group will be on full alert until the danger is past at which time they will return to their feeding activities. If on the other hand the warning growl is followed by a loud cough, the sounder will leave the scene and not return for some time. If the flight also includes the sharp exhaling of breath, akin to air brakes on a heavy goods lorry, the flight will turn into one of blind panic. The sound appears to signify real and immediate danger and the boar act as one and flee the scene hot foot.

Observing boar in this way has provided a deep insight into the behaviour of feeding boar and not just confined to activities within a sounder. My observations have extended to exploring the relationships across sounders. What becomes clear is that the dominance hierarchy within a sounder also applies across sounders. So for example, if one group of animals were on the feeding site and the site was approached by another less dominant group, the less dominant group would remain in the undergrowth some distance away from the site until the dominant group had left. In the opposite scenario the dominant group would come straight into the site without hesitation and the less dominant group, having sensed the arriving group would have already left.

To observe wild boar on a feeding sight in any sort of detail you need to be:

(i)   reasonably close to the action.

(ii) Out of sight; although the boar has poor eyesight it can still spot movement at a reasonable distance.

(iii) Far enough away to flex and get comfortable; boar hearing is second to none and can pick up the slightest sound, that of pouring coffee, a sneeze or a belch, etc will be picked up by the boar and recognised as unnatural and therefore cause for alarm. One death knell for any wildlife study is the sound of a Velcro fastener which I have found to my cost on many an occasion. Everything we purchase these days seems to be festooned with those dreaded hook and loop fasteners. If boar pick up such a sound they may just run off a few yards, stop and listen for a repeat (pardon the pun) which, if heard would raise the alarm level further and they will be gone possibly for the night. If no follow up sound is detected they will likely return to the feed almost at once. To reduce the risk of bolting the horses or boar in this case and in the worst case ruin an entire evening, I removed all Velcro fastenings from my gear. A pain but a necessary one.

(iv) Take up a downwind position; the slightest scent of danger the boar will be gone and the scent of human beings, in the early days of my study, was associated with danger. The problem is with a hide close enough to be able to film and study the boar behaving normally all the above issues are present. With a hide on the ground twigs and brambles are going to get in the way and noise is inevitable. Wind around the site is rarely constant and whatever care one takes to get upwind it won't be too long before one finds oneself downwind and the scent picked up. They are on constant alert and will not settle down to feed normally while such scent is in the air. This makes for a lot of wasted time and effort for the observer.

I put up with this frustration for sometime but finally came to the conclusion that a hide on the ground was not the answer, of course I needed a high seat. I figured it needed to be far enough off the ground so that the boar would not be able to see nor smell me. Provided that I sat still neither would they hear me, at least that was the idea. To test the theory out I borrowed a high seat from a friend. It worked perfectly. I was able to film wild boar completely at home and relaxed oblivious to my presence. To boot here was a very comfortable seat for myself.

So, I set about constructing a lightweight aluminium seat that I could easily move around the area as and from one site to another. Once the high seat was in position it was just a matter of blending the seat in with its surroundings. Mostly I used branches and other material from the site. Sometimes I had to drape a large camouflage net over the whole thing to be sure that it could not be seen by the boar. A hand rail round the top of the seat afforded a convenient anchorage for a camera clamp.

Rock steady filming and a freed up pair of hands to observe what was going on around the area through a pair of binoculars. The one draw back was the tendency to be watching one scene while the camera filmed something elsewhere. Moving the camera around from scene to scene can result in an awful lot of poorly composed shots but overall I was happy with the film I took. I did miss some great scenes off camera that I wished I had recorded but there you go, you can't have everything. One time I was watching a group of boar feeding and was filming the squabbles between the yearlings. Whilst the camera filmed this scene, I was simultaneously watching a group of piglets play fighting just off camera – something that went on every time the sounder came in to feed and not at all out of the ordinary. The older the piglets get the less time they spend playing and the more time is spent searching for food. The three piglets in question had been playfully testing each other's strength. There was no one boar winning out in this play, until that is the sounder was joined by the most senior member of the group with her piglets who for some reason was late coming in. Now these piglets were senior, and therefore dominant over those already there. One of these piglets, a young male, stood watching the three at play for a few moments, then having made up his mind, approached the three with his bristles up and knocked all three off their feet in one swift movement. He then turned and walked away as if nothing had happened. The three piglets that had been playing stared on in a kind of "what the hell was all that about?" fashion as he walked away. Not one of them was up for following and taking him on. That put an end to the play for a while. This one incident alone shows how important the dominance thing is even at such an early age. The three youngsters would certainly remember the incident.

Once at a site my standard procedure was to first locate the high seat in a suitable tree. Large conifers are ideal for this purpose. The branches on these trees, if the tree is close to the edge of the wood or overlooking a clearing, reach almost down to ground level and provide a natural screen. In this case very little additional cover is necessary. Being a belt and braces man, I felt I always tended to overdo the cover. My priority was first class film and I comforted myself with the thought that the extra effort was always worthwhile.

Another advantage being in a high seat is that you are able to observe what's going on in the area around the seat as well as on the feed site itself. Something that is not possible on the ground due to the undergrowth. Once the seat was installed it was then just a matter of putting enough food down to gain the boars' attention. Sometimes in the first couple of years of my study, this could take a few weeks before the boar found the feed, but once found the boar would come to the site on a regular basis.

The need to be cautious

I started to feed from about the end of February on a weekly basis putting food down both Saturday and Sunday and by the end of March the boar were usually coming to the site every night to check for food. Once the clocks changed at the end of March I would then feed every night, rain or shine. Leaving my car about three kilometres from the feed area, I would walk into the area taking care not to disturb the laying up areas used by the boar. This meant that I had to cross some private land to get to my selected sight. On reaching the site area I would first check to make sure I wasn't disturbing early arrivals, put the food down and then leave the same way that I had come so as not to spook boar making their way to the site. In all the round trip was about 4.5 miles and would usually take about an hour and a quarter. I had found that if I parked in the same spot on a regular basis then my feeding site would soon be compromised and I would have to move sites and start again somewhere else. There were occasions when I was aware of being followed as soon as I left home. A vehicle would appear from a side road and stay with me. Knowing my pursuers were more concerned about time than I was, I would double back, sometimes return to the house, pop into a friend's house and on many occasions simply lose them. The price of a wild boar carcase in those early days was about four times that of venison which made it very attractive pocket money. These people looked for a quick in and out and not a lengthy extraction of a dead boar. Hard work was to be avoided. My newly selected site was perfect for the purpose and over the eight years that I used this site I never lost one animal to poachers.

A further development in boar poaching was the introduction of specially bred dogs. These boar dogs are of a heavy lurcher variety with a considerable amount of pit bull in the blood line yielding courage, determination and aggression to the final offspring. These dogs are capable of bringing down an adult fallow buck on their own and when used against boar are fitted with leather waistcoats studded with pointed metal rivets, to protect the dogs from the sharp tusks of the boar once it has been brought to bay. When the animal being pursued stops and turns to defend itself it is said to be brought to bay.

Deer tend to flee until they can run no more and only then do they turn to face their pursuers. Boar on the other hand quite like to mix it and will turn and face the opposition much sooner. I am informed that these dogs are now fetching a high price in certain circles. Apathy on the part of the national authorities has left current regulations with little or no teeth. Pretty much anything goes. It is no surprise whatsoever that boar dogs have arrived on the scene. Free range boar baiting is back with the apparent blessing of the powers that be. Wild boar remain at the mercy of unscrupulous people throughout the year,

Difficult to control

The fact that nearly all the viable breeding populations of free living wild boar have established themselves on publicly owned property is no surprise. These vast areas of forest are the perfect hiding place for the boar. That these places are open to the public 24/7, 365 days a year it is equally unsurprising that problems will arise. Policing these forests is an impossible task given the number of full-time forestry staff at an all-time low. Unsavoury individuals have relative freedom to undertake, at the very least, frowned upon activities under cover of the forest. The trespass laws are limited on land that open to the public and prosecution of offenders is uncommon due to legal limitations. Privately owned woodland on the other hand is a different matter and due to the game laws and the "trespass in pursuit of" etc. there is more chance of a prosecution being successful. Increasingly, however, the police and crown prosecution service are reluctant to get involved, and landowners who have pressed charges find themselves on occasion at the receiving end of revenge attacks. Vehicles stolen or damaged, arson attacks in some cases with damage caused running into hundreds of thousands of pounds to name but a few. Inevitably there results a reluctance to press charges. Poaching in medieval times was a serious offence and punishable in most cases by imprisonment and in some cases by death. Another punishment was of course transportation to the Van Diemen's Land known today as Tasmania and from there to Australia and a life of hard labour. There are some people today who wish that both these options were still available to us!

Loveable rogue or just rogue

Unfortunately poaching today has lost its romantic image of the one for the pot country rogue who knew every tree that would hold a pheasant, or where to find a rabbit or hare. The old fashioned poachers were satisfied with pheasant, rabbit and hare. All easy to obtain and conceal. Apart from the rabbit, the old fashioned poacher's family very rarely got to eat the proceeds of a night's work. Why would they? The proceeds from the sale of a brace of pheasants would feed the family for a week. The birds themselves would provide but one meal. This type of old fashioned countryman who just needed to feed his family has now been replaced by large gangs of professionals who make a living out of poaching, and a good one to. Venison and wild boar are their main targets. These same professional gangs will also be found hare coursing where large sums of money change hands on the outcome of a single run. A coordinated operation by two or three gangs in different parts of the county at the same time has the authorities chasing their tails with rarely a culprit caught. The problem has become so serious in some parts of the country that farmers and landowners have formed early warning groups to inform one another of suspicious goings on in an attempt to combat the problem.

Patience

To photograph or study any form of wildlife patience is a prerequisite; to sit quite still for long periods of time in, what can be, most unpleasant conditions is not easy. In normal quiet and undisturbed conditions, wildlife will immediately be aware of an alien arrival. The atmosphere within the wood will change, birds will be the first to announce your presence, normally wrens or blue tits will be the first to scold you as you move through the wood. This scolding will be picked up by other birds and mammals within hearing distance. This state of alertness will continue until you have settled. I have come to the conclusion that an area of woodland takes about 20 to 25 minutes to settle down after the perceived threat has passed. Up to this point the wildlife will be on the lookout for danger from all directions. Birds will be the first to signal that the danger has passed and inform the rest of the woodland that all appears well again. They will start to sing and call and return to their normal routines. A sudden movement, cough or sneeze will betray your presence and the alert process starts once more.

Hunting the wren

The wren is steeped in legend and folklore as being the king of all birds. There are still areas today, on St Steven's Day as part of the Christmas celebrations, the Hunting the Wren Festival takes place. The legend has it that the wren was responsible for the capture and subsequent death of a medieval king by betraying his hiding place in the heather by its constant scolding. This led the king's pursuers directly to his hiding place.

Mammals, like boar, deer, foxes, badgers, and particularly squirrels listen out for just such warnings and are quick to pass on the news to all within ear shot. Once seated in my high seat it was not unusual to note the presence of both squirrel and blue tit or wren in the adjacent trees. Just as the boar, after a short while, they came to accept that my presence represented no danger. In fact the squirrels benefited at times from the feed put down for the boar. Sometimes the mixture contained peanuts if I was lucky enough to obtain a bag that was past its best. I included a handful or two in the mixture; the piglets loved them and so did the squirrels! The squirrels would sit in the trees overlooking the feed site, and once the feed was down and I had retired to my perch, they would descend and check it out. If there were peanuts included they would help themselves to as much of this bounty as they could before the boar turned up. Sometimes as many as five at a time appeared as if by magic for the feast. But all the while one would be keeping a close watch to see that I remained no threat. That the squirrels and foxes took advantage of my free meals provided me with an early warning system that the boar were on their way. Foxes have acute hearing and they would stop feeding, prick their ears and look in the direction of the approaching boar, making their leave before the boar arrived. They always knew long before I did that the boar were coming in.

From time to time I could get hold of several 20kg bags of dry dog food. This was added to the mixture that went down for the boar. This proved especially appealing to the foxes, they would search the area meticulously for all the pieces of dried meat and consume as much as they could. When they could eat no more they'd collect as much as they could in their mouths and trot off into the woodland to bury their surpluses and return again and again until the boar arrived. It amused me to see the boar with their acute sense of smell, sniff out these caches that the foxes had so carefully hidden. A justifiable act I suppose given the food was intended for them.

The foxes maintained a discreet and cautious distance when the piglets first appeared with their mothers. The adult boars would drive the foxes away if they dared to venture too close, but once the piglets had grown in size and confidence, the adults were less protective of the youngsters. The piglets would treat the whole thing as a game and chase the foxes away every time they tried to come into feed. The foxes would use their cunning to try to outwit the piglets by coming in from a different direction only for another piglet to join in the game and chase the intruder away. What would have happened if the fox had stood his ground I do not know. The situation never arose during my observations of the feeding site. But I would expect the sows would then have intervened to afford protection for their piglets.

Supplementary feeding

With bags of whole maize at between eight and 10lbs and poultry feed and mixed corn similarly priced, a few bags of peanuts deemed unfit for human consumption and dog food past its sell by date, made a welcome addition to my feed supply not to mention a sigh of relief from my wallet. Feeding, as I was every night, amounted to about 75kg of food a week – quite a drain on my income. So I was ever grateful when I got a call from a very good friend to ask if I would like some of this reject feed. Over the years it saved me a considerable amount of money; I doubt if I could have continued my research without this generous gesture. My then companion Jack Russell, Jessica, struggled with the idea that food which by rights should be in her bowl beside the fire was being thrown down out here in the woods where any creature could help itself. She felt a need to express her dissatisfaction with this and every now and then would sneak a mouthful when she thought I wasn't looking only to give the game away by looking very sheepish once the deed was done.

Once the nights were light enough, I had the added burden of cameras and recording gear to carry with the feed, a total weight of about 2.5 stone (16kg). Hard going but I didn't begrudge it. The amount of food put down varied from week to week to accord with the size and number of animals coming to feed. The first animals to find the feed were usually youngsters from last year who, being less cautious than the older more experienced animals, tended to let their belly rule their heads. Usually I could hear them coming which gave me a chance to switch the camera in readiness. As the evening wore on and the light started to fade then the older animals would turn up and the youngsters would give way to the adults who would clear up what food was left. The youngsters were actively driven away from the site on occasions.

After about two to three weeks of feeding at the site the boar became used to my scent and were not unduly alarmed when approaching the feeding area if they caught my scent. However, if someone else were to cross the site or feed on my behalf, the boar would stand back in the trees and survey the area for some time before venturing any closer. By the time the nights were light enough to film up to around nine or 10 the boar had come to accept me as part of the furniture. Provided I didn't make any sudden moves my presence was tolerated. Guard duty continued though with one of them on constant alert, and every few minutes would stare directly at the tree where my high seat was located. Wild boar cannot look upwards as can deer or foxes. Constant movement of the head whilst rooting for food causes build-up of heavy muscle in the neck. The muscles become very strong, strong enough in some cases to lift another adult right off the ground in one movement. This muscularity effects a block to lifting the head above horizontal and so prevents them from looking up.

This trust in the feeding area is what allows the animals to relax and behave normally. It was always this that took the most time to achieve, but once this was achieved the boar would readily come onto the feed site, sometimes there before I had managed to climb the 15 feet to my seat in the trees. Another thing worth mentioning is the need for concealment in the form of clothing. I always wore camouflage of one sort or another. It was most important to cover hands and face. The sudden sight of a white hand or face was enough to end the session for the night.

Weekend visitors

As it got lighter and the dog walker numbers increased, I would stop filming at weekends. From Easter time onwards the boar were reluctant to leave the shelter of their laying up areas until the woods were quiet again so trying to film at weekends was normally a waste of time. The food went down just the same; it was essential that the boar found food each time they visited the site to keep them coming.

On occasion due to illness, or other commitments, I would call on one of my very good friends to feed. It was very good of them. On occasion they too were able to obtain footage of the boar themselves. I was let down by one person who took it upon himself to take visitors with him. It took a week after this foolishness for the boar to begin to trust the site again though they still remained nervous for a long while after this. Eventually things got back to a normal routine. Needless to say that person is no longer a friend. After this episode, I called upon friends whose discretion was beyond doubt.

Once a regular routine of feeding was established I was able to predict with some confidence when the boar would appear. It allowed me to then work out what had been going on in the area during the day.

If the woodland had been disturbed in any way during the day the boar would arrive late on feed. Mondays would see the boar waiting until almost dark which indicated that the forest had been heavily visited by people, e.g. dog walkers, over the weekend. As the week progressed the arrival times would get earlier and by Thursday night the boar would be on site early evening sometimes waiting for me to put the food down.

There was never enough food put down to cause the boar to become dependent on it, difficult though this could be to judge.

Their welfare was always my prime concern. I would have been signing a boar's death warrant if I allowed it to become dependent.

The adults were now coming to feed with the yearlings and were consuming most of the feed. As soon as the youngsters' heads dropped to feed, the adults would threat charge and chase them away only for the youngsters to return almost at once to the site where they would be subjected to another threat charge. Youngsters returning a third time would receive not a threat but the real thing. The adult would press home the attack and on occasion the youngster would not come back to the site for some time. Eventually the sight of all that food right in front of it would be too much and it would start all over again.

The adults in question were by now quite clearly pregnant sows and by their shape and behaviour close to farrowing. This would account for their aggressive behaviour and their increased appetite. They were eager to consume as much food as they could to ready themselves for the nesting period with their piglets. They may not feed for several days, maybe two weeks with some sows not taking any food at all. Each pregnant sow, in order of dominance would leave the site with just a few days in between each departure and they would remain absent. The sounder continued as normal with the food being consumed by those that remained.

Ten days away

After about 10 days of peace and quiet by which time their piglets were strong enough, the sows would return to the feeding site. Under cover of the surrounding woodland they would bring their piglets to within a short distance of the feeding site and leave them there until they were sure that the site was safe for the vulnerable young piglets just a few days old. The piglets would remain under cover just where the sow had left them, their stripy coats making it impossible to see them against the leaves and branches comprising the woodland floor. Unless you happen to see them arrive with the sow with this camouflage it was impossible to pick them out. This precautionary routine was followed for several days. When all was clear, the sow would usher them in and they would soon settle in with the rest of the group and begin to search for morsels of food. Their snouts would go down as soon as they reached the feeding area, something they would do for the rest of their life. Their snouts are on the go all the time unless they are at play or in flight. Once the piglets appeared on site I would change the feed mixture to include some poultry feed pellets containing a high level of protein which the piglets seemed to favour. They chased about looking for these tasty morsels. Squabbles would break out on a regular basis as they sought to establish a pecking order amongst themselves. Although dependent on mother's milk, the piglets start to pick up morsels of food as soon as they are strong enough to follow the sows on their nightly wanderings. By the time the youngsters are eight weeks old they are able to support themselves, becoming less dependent on mum. Although they still remain with the sounder they progressively become more independent.

This year's baby sitters

So the sows that remained after the exodus of the pregnant females were to be the nannies, a duty that the experienced sows and the young females performed every year. The young males play no part in this baby sitting at all. Their sole interest is to consume as much food as possible and if this necessitated pushing the piglets out of the way to get it so be it. But woe betide any young male that became too aggressive with the piglets. He would be in for a severe reprimand by the females. On one occasion I witnessed two sows admonish an offender who had made a piglet squeal and drive him out of the wood altogether. His own squeals could be heard as the sows pursued him. That particular young male was never allowed to feed with the rest of the sounder on that site again. He would approach to within 25 metres only to be rebuffed by the unforgiving females. The piglet that was hurt in this instance was not seen again. Its mother continued to come in, bringing her remaining piglet with her. With just the two to begin with this was a big loss to her.

This particular year the sounder comprised five adult sows and their 10 offspring from the previous year only produced five piglets between them. There had been 14 offspring but four were lost over the autumn and winter when they would have been eight or nine months old, an ideal size for the freezer.

There were times when a sow would bring her piglets close to the feed site and for whatever reason found things not to her liking immediately. Sometimes they would not return to this particular feeding area at all that year, certainly not in daylight anyway. Sows are devoted to their piglets. As they get older the sows become even more alert to possible danger, more streetwise I would say. Senior members of the sounder will rarely venture out with their piglets until after dark preferring to remain under cover during the day. Even on moonlit nights the sows stay close to cover at all times unless they are moving between woods. This caution extends to younger sows as well. I have seen sows with piglets at foot approach a feed site, stop just short of the area and after viewing the scene for a while, take their well-grown piglets away only to return a half hour later from the other side of the site, a journey of considerable distance through thick cover. This was done solely to avoid moving their offspring from one side of the feed site to the other in the open. I had unintentionally scattered the feed nearer to one side of the area than the other, and even though the distance to be covered was only 20 yards, the sow was unprepared to take the risk. When foraging in open areas for worms and grubs boar will stay close to the edge of the woodland. The comfort of nearby cover of trees and bushes is a necessary condition for boar to relax sufficiently. They must feel confident that they can retreat quickly to cover should danger threaten. They will venture out into the open only in total darkness and once they feel secure.

Another incident which illustrates a sow's devotion as a mother occurred one night whilst we were driving through the forest after dark. We spotted a young sow standing on the edge of the wood, just a little bit back from the road. We had gone past her before we knew she was there. We turned the vehicle round as soon as we could and drove back the way we had just come. The sow was still there in the same place beside the road. We stopped the vehicle and turned the engine off to see what she would do. After a short while she moved into the road and across to the other side where she put her head through a hole in the fence and stood listening for a few seconds. She then returned to the middle of the road and gave a soft grunt whereupon five piglets clambered down the bank and crossed the road followed by two more sows. All this time the first sow stood in the middle of the road, rather like a lollipop lady seeing young children across a road. So fascinated were we that despite having four cameras in the vehicle, we never managed one single photograph!

My feeding site for that first full year of study was in an area of mature conifers which was dissected by a high voltage power line. The area under the power lines was cleared of trees every six or seven years by the power company. In between these clearances the bracken and brambles flourished and in some places were as high as six or seven feet; perfect cover for the sows and piglets. Anyone foolhardy enough to try to penetrate this jungle would be detected immediately and the boar would move out of the way before the intruder had got five yards. This wall of vegetation gave my feed site the perfect screen from prying eyes and ensured that the area was not disturbed. It was while sitting in my high seat in this location one evening that I realised just how important it was to safely site the seat. I suspect a health and safety officer would have had a fit if he or she had seen me sitting as I was 14 feet off the ground on a metal seat, under a fir tree, which in turn was no more than 15 feet from the power lines and in a raging thunderstorm. With thunder cracking all around and lightening continually splitting the night, I thought to myself that I had probably had better ideas in my time. One saving grace, I was only observing, not filming on this particular evening and didn't have too much gear with me. A hasty exit to a safer place was called for and executed as fast as I could, no drier but somewhat less hazardous.

The animals in that first study group were of a uniform colour all showing the dark characteristics of the European animals from which they are descended. It soon became clear the animals that were coming to my feeding site were of two different family groups or sounders with one group dominant over the other. I had quite by accident elected to feed on the boundary between the two groups. This became apparent when the boar were on feed and by the nervousness of the sub dominant group.

Alpha male

At this time although I had seen plenty of adult sows, I had not seen an alpha male but then I was assured by Mr M that he did not exist. He believed at that time that all males had free access to all females. He also informed me that it would not be possible to identify the farm from which the boar had originally escaped by way of DNA tests. This was because, he had told me, there was no control specimen with which to compare.

Call me simple but I could not follow this reasoning. Maybe I'm over-sensitive but I was sure I was getting the "country bumpkin" treatment. "You couldn't possibly understand it's all a bit technical." What I did know was that it had been possible to confirm from blood and tissue samples collected that they were for the most part definitely pure wild boar of the French variety, with a few samples showing Eastern European extraction. So, I reasoned, if it was possible to distinguish western and eastern boar, why not the parentage of the boar that were now roaming free in the British countryside?

If the feeding site was to be used for the purposes of shooting then the food would be deployed in one of the following ways:

(1) a single pile in the centre of a large clearing,
(2) or the corner of a field known to be used by boar as a foraging area or crossing point from one piece of woodland to another.

The object of such deployment is to encourage the boar to move into a suitable position for a successful shot, and hopefully a clean kill. This unfortunately is not always the case and it is not unusual to see an animal carrying an injury of one sort or another.

Responsible hunting

Most people who stalk on a regular basis follow the regulations as laid down in the various acts of parliament that govern deer stalking, e.g. the size or calibre of rifle or shotgun using solid slug ammunition. Failure to comply can result in the offender's firearms licence being withdrawn. Stalkers are also required to take a proficiency test to ensure competency. That is not the case for wild boar. There are no such regulations. Most who pursue wild boar for sport do so responsibly and use a suitable weapon, one that is large enough to do the job required without causing the animal any pain or unnecessary stress. The object being one shot one clean kill.

Not everyone is blessed with such a responsible attitude and these will use any means at their disposal including the use of snares, shotguns loaded with totally unsuitable ammunition, or even crossbows. The latter being quiet is the weapon of choice for poachers operating close to buildings.

Animals turn up at the game dealer with shotgun wounds which have become infected and in some cases gangrenous which means that the carcase is condemned as unfit for human consumption. However, not all carcases are sold through a reputable dealer. Some enter the food chain through the back door shops without proper inspection. One would think that no self respecting proprietor would risk serving uncertified food to their customers but lack of regulation of wild boar means the potential is there.

Venison served in eateries is traceable back to the point of origin, from the moment it is shot to the point of sale. Unscrupulous behaviour can therefore be policed. Sadly this is not the case for wild boar.

Pest species

We have a close season for deer, pheasant, partridge, grouse and other wildfowl, salmon and trout all of which are plentiful. Wild boar, however, are classed as a pest species by the powers that be and as a result there is no close season with regard to hunting and shooting them despite them numbering less than 3,000. Does that make sense and is that a responsible attitude to be taken by the Government? Is that what they believe to be animal welfare? How can it be right to be allowed to shoot a sow who is pregnant and about to give birth or for that matter, one that has already given birth to her litter. Who cares for the piglets? Too young and they will starve, a terrible death. If they are lucky and not too large, a fox will find them and put them out of their agony,

I was once asked by a television producer during filming about my thoughts on the plight of the boar. I replied, "There are countries where it is perfectly legal to purchase suckling pig for the table. In this country, our stance on animal welfare has rightly led to prohibition of such. And yet present legislation permits unlimited shooting of wild boar piglets. How can we sleep easily at night?" When the programme was broadcast my answer was severely edited and implied that "it was OK to go out and shoot as many as you like as there is nothing to stop you". I learned a big lesson from that experience. Keep answers brief and simple.

Wild boar numbers

During the winter of 1999-2000 boar numbers were high. The previous winter's crop of acorns and chestnuts was very light which resulted in a large number of young females being unable to gain enough weight to become sexually mature. Therefore a large number of females were now 18 months and ready to mate. By the end of October the forest seemed to be full of boar. There was sign everywhere you looked together with the sound of squabbling boar in almost every patch of dense undergrowth. At one stage in early November at the beginning of the rut, there were 45 breeding animals on one feed site in Beckley Forest, a figure that has never been repeated. With such a large number of boar in the area it was bound to attract attention and the poachers descended on the area in numbers. So much so that by the end of January it was difficult to find sign of boar anywhere. During that autumn of 1999 an area of mixed woodland in Bixley Woods part of an area managed by Sussex Wildlife Trust comprising some five acres of mature oak, chestnut, birch and hornbeam, was turned over completely in one night by foraging boar searching for acorns and other fruits. A veritable boar army was at work to achieve this sort of devastation.

The man from the ministry

That winter the man from "M" was busy with his traps again and had a number of animals with radio tags attached, only this time they were less conspicuous. He was able to follow them successfully for some while without too much trouble. He was however having problems with other animals springing the traps before the boar, usually badgers. He was catching badgers every night in one trap or another. He would release them only to catch them again a few nights later! This was occurring in two particular areas so he decided to move his traps to a different area. It was while siting one of these traps that he found himself in a bit of a predicament. The trap he was setting up had a fault on the treadle that released the door; it was too stiff and did not work properly so running repairs were needed. He set the door of the trap in the open position and climbed inside to attend to the sticking mechanism. The door had a safety device that secured it in the open position which he had forgotten to engage. The result of this omission was that the treadle, when tested, worked perfectly, and he'd managed to trap himself. Now these traps were designed to make it impossible to open them from the inside. The catches that locked the door in the shut position were impossible to get at from the inside. To make matters worse it was early afternoon and he was working alone. He had a mobile phone with him but the reception was patchy and the only number that he could reach was that of the local game dealer who was out tending his sheep. Finally after three and a half hours he managed to summon help. The game dealer had a thoroughly enjoyable time as he released Mr M from his self-imposed confinement. Needless to say his imprisonment had already been relayed throughout the community. Any official such as M is not exactly welcomed in the country communities, he and the likes of him, are viewed with suspicion and mistrust. Any opportunity to disrupt or even sabotage his efforts were seized upon so the chance to ridicule the official was met with equal relish. This incident with the trap was the butt of many a joke in the local pubs for some while.

The man from the ministry had by now acquired a full-time female assistant. Some blokes have all the luck. She was an extremely attractive girl who now took over most of his mundane duties such as radio tracking at night and the mapping of the areas that were frequented by the boar for laying up and foraging. She would spend hours on her own in various locations studying patches of ground a yard square at a time. Mr M on the other hand was spending more and more time on other tasks, travelling to other parts of the country to investigate other sightings of wild boar. One of these sightings in 1998 was of a boar that had been seen on the outskirts of the Forest of Dean. He had been asked to investigate on behalf of the Forestry Commission who manage the area. The last thing they wanted was wild boar roaming free in the forest. Its vast acreage would make it almost impossible to eradicate them if they became established. There were boar farms in the area and the boar had been seen within a mile of one of these. After driving round the area for a few days and finding no sign of the animal, he declared the forest to be boar free which he later conceded had been a little premature. He returned to East Anglia to his swan counting or whatever it was that he did when not studying wild boar on the Kent and Sussex border. My response to this bit of information was as follows. If the boar was seen that close to the forest there is almost certainly more than one and once established in the forest it will be almost impossible to remove them. Boar can be present in an area for several years before their activities are noticed. The rooting activities of the boar are quite often mistaken for that of badgers and to the untrained eye the disruption can look identical but once the two are compared side by side the difference becomes obvious. The object of all this attention is of course the humble earthworm, both boar and badger consume an awful lot of them.

There is one estate in particular on the Kent and Sussex border that has suffered more than most as far as rooting by boar is concerned, the staff are constantly trying to patch up the areas of rooting in newly planted woodland. The fields were originally small grass fields that were no longer economical to work due to their size so the decision was taken to plant them up with trees. These fields were visited on a regular basis by the boar in their search for earthworms.

The results of this worming in these fields by the boar means that now in order to mow the grass the estate now has to use tillage equipment to level out the fields two or three times a year. Quite often this is done during a period of dry weather so as to let the machines work without problems, the effect of this is to create an ideal tilth in which the worms etc thrive and so the whole thing has to be done again and again and so on. It must be very frustrating for the estate manager to return to an area that had been levelled and rolled 24 hours ago only to find that the boar have turned it over again. This sort of activity does not seem to occur as much on arable land as it does on pasture due I believe to the fact that arable land is constantly being worked and the worms and grubs are less concentrated. The same thing applies to newly sown pasture, without the root mass of permanent pasture the concentration of food items is diminished and the effort required to get at them outweighs the benefit.

Cannibalism

Whilst on the subject of food I will return to the matter of cannibalism. It is not pleasant to think of our animals being in the habit of consuming their own kind but unfortunately it is a fact of life in the animal world, wild boar being no exception. I have two examples of this within my study. First, there was the case of a three-year-old pregnant sow that was shot on a piece of land on the edge of a farrowing wood round about Christmas time and, for whatever reason, was not collected but moved into the wood from where she fell. She had been bled, by which I mean that she had her throat cut after death to drain as much blood as possible. An attempt had also been made to remove her intestines. At this stage she had been abandoned, possibly the perpetrators had been disturbed and she was left in the wood in a depression. In fact in one of the holes left by the extraction of iron ore by the Romans. The fact that she was pregnant was easy to see, the part-developed piglets were clearly visible. The carcass was first found by the usual scavengers a couple of days after the sow was shot. The footprints of fox and badger were clearly visible in the soft soil in the bottom of the hole. The weather was cold and frosty so the carcass had not yet started to decay but there was enough smell to attract the foxes and badgers. Twenty four hours later the scene had changed completely. There were now no signs of fox or badger at all only that of boar and the remains were now mostly pieces of back bone and the skin and head, the rest had been eaten. The soft mud showed clearly the foot prints of wild boar with their distinctive dew claws giving the game away. All this happened at a time when there was plenty of natural food available to the boar so the predation was not a result of hunger. The sow concerned was one of my study group and I had followed her first litter the year before. I was looking forward to see if she would improve on her litter size the next year. She would have tipped the scales at around 80kg and all this was consumed by the rest of her sounder in 24 hours. Allowing for the hours of daylight when the boar are not active, this would leave about 16 hours maximum.

The second incident occurred some nine months later when a yearling sow that had been driven out of the sounder, died either from disease or starvation brought on by disease. For some reason the rest of the group would not let her back into the sounder after she gave birth although she had been running with the rest of her family quite happily all through the spring. In fact she was one of the more dominant youngsters from the year before, so much so that she was the only one of the yearling females from the group to get pregnant, the rest of her sisters and cousins being empty. Of the five adult sows in the sounder only three of those were pregnant. These three were with piglets at foot when the youngster in question failed to appear on feed one night. She had been on feed the night before and was her normal dominant self, making sure she got her share. What was unusual was that she left the feed site quite some time before the rest. She would normally stay until there was not a scrap of food left. This I have discovered is quite normal behaviour for a female about to give birth.

It was two weeks to the day that I next saw her, she had clearly given birth, her shape had changed, she no longer had the tell tale sign that she was pregnant. She did not have piglets with her when she arrived, but she did show signs that she was feeding piglets. It is not unusual for mothers to leave their piglets safely tucked away somewhere out of sight. Hunger was her driving force; she came into the feeding site at a fast lope and her head went down as soon as she arrived. Two of her relatives immediately set about her and drove her away from the food. The same thing happened each time she tried to get back in and this went on for about 45 minutes until she gave up trying and left the scene followed by two of the adult sows who were not feeding piglets. She never tried to come in to feed while the rest of the sounder were there again. She would approach to within sight of the feed site, and wait until the rest of her relatives had gone before coming in. I never saw her piglets so cannot say how many she had. What I can say is that when she first returned after her two-week absence there were just two teats in use so at that time she was feeding two. What happened to them I do not know but that female was never allowed to rejoin the sounder and was driven away every time she came into contact with them.

This female was a well-liked member of the sounder before the incident and, on one occasion when she was late on feed, some 15 minutes after the rest, she was welcomed by two of her sisters as though she was a long lost relative. What her crime was I do not know. The next time I saw her was several weeks later. She was a shadow of her former self, a pitiful sight, almost unable to walk and was just lying in the middle of a field, about a hundred yards from the safety of the woodland, I could have run up to her and caught her if I had wanted to she was in that bad a way. I never saw her alive again after that, but I did find her body some five days later, or what was left of it, the rest of the sounder had found it first. Although the head was recognisable there was not much left of the animal that I had watched the year before when she came into feed as a piglet. I had watched her develop into the teenager in her second year and had been in the first group of animals to find the feed site. It was very sad.

So any suggestion that boar or pigs in general will only feed on there own kind when they are desperate is simply untrue.

Adult males and indeed females will at times kill and eat nests of piglets if they find them. The reason for this is that if the male is not the father of the piglets then by killing them it will quickly bring the sow back into breeding condition again and provided he is not driven off by a more dominant boar he will then father her next litter. This is the main reason that the sows leave the rest of the sounder and find an isolated spot to have their youngsters, even avoiding their own sisters, who if given the chance, would act similarly to give there own piglets a better chance and a step up in dominance. Once the sows have piglets of their own the danger is past, and the females will look out for the youngsters as if they were their own even when the piglets are quite independent. One of the adult sows will be close by to alert the youngsters to danger should it arise. She may not be visible but she will be there within earshot of them. The relationship between the females and their piglets is so sensitive that the sows will detect a health problem in any of their offspring. They have been known to starve youngsters to death if the condition is terminal. The sows will not waste any effort in producing milk for a piglet that is not going to survive; the welfare of the rest of her young is her priority. Only the fittest will survive, it's just nature's way of ensuring that the species continue to thrive. Harsh maybe but necessary.

Above: The boar that fell in the pond. *Below:* This is the sort of damage that gives the boar a bad name, the result of boar rooting for earth worms.

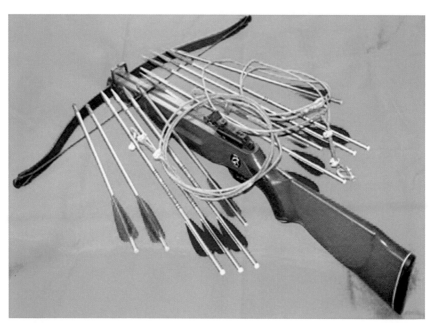

Above: Tools of the poaching trade, crossbow and heavy duty snares all of which are strictly illegal. *Below:* The result of boar worming on a woodland ride.

Above: Boar wallow, Beckley, East Sussex. *Below:* Boar tracks in the mud.

Above: *Sows and piglets on feed site in Beckley forest, East Sussex.*
Below: *Caught out on the wrong side of the fence..*

*Above: Rabbit burrow destroyed by boar searching for acorns. Jessica is only in the picture as a guide to the size of the destruction. **Below:** The result of too much brandy on your damsons, aggresson begins to rise.*

Above: Wild boar tucking into damsons soaked in brandy. *Below:* The after effects of too much brandy, a headache.

Above: Two man high seat set on the edge of a woodland clearing.
Below: Fox cubs take advantage of a free meal.

Above: The results of boar rooting for a nest of young rabbits. *Below:* Wild boar at night on a feed site in West Sussex.

Above: *Yearling boar on a feed site in an oak wood in East Sussex.*
Below: *Typical boar rooting along the edge of a wood in East Sussex.*

Above: This idyllic picture of a sow and piglets is not what it seems. The sow in question is fact a dormant female and in this instance is acting as a baby sitter to four separate litters of piglets belonging to more senior members of the sounder. **Below:** Six feet high boar proof fence (and every other mammal as well).

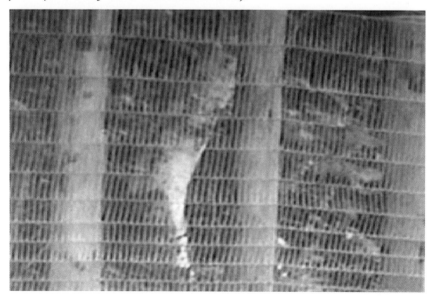

Chapter Four

Media Interest

A FTER MY success filming wild boar from a high seat, I had obtained several hours of good quality video footage, good enough for television to use, and they did on a number of occasions use film shot by me in Kent and East Sussex. What I think attracted the media in the first place was all my film was shot in the wild and perhaps because it was by a complete beginner. The national newspapers also took a keen interest and sent several reporters down to Kent to find out more about what boar were doing in the countryside. Most of these reporters were genuinely interested in what was happening and were keen to learn more about the wild boar, their affect on the flora and fauna and such like. Some on the other hand were only after sensational headlines, how many people had been injured, how many sheep and cattle had been slain by these marauding beasts, and news of a certain pop star who lived locally who was harbouring these beasts and releasing them into the wild. On being informed that none of these things were actually happening, these types just printed what they fancied never letting the truth get in the way of a good story. This poor reporting extended to selective use of interviews with myself and sometimes downright misquotes. I spent many a time explaining just what I had said to readers of these dreadful articles.

Having filmed the boar all that previous year from the same spot I began to look for a new area for the forthcoming year to compare the behaviour of boar in different locations. I found a suitable location within the same area of forest but this time was within the wood, totally enclosed by conifers and deciduous trees. This meant that once the trees were in full leaf light levels made it more difficult to film. The high seat needed a lot more effort to conceal with vegetation and camouflage netting necessary to make a good job of it. Just how good, I was to find out whilst waiting for boar to turn up one warm evening. There were quite a few people about on this particular Saturday evening and the boar not surprisingly were late coming into feed, the boar laying up until walkers, dogs, horse riders etc headed for home and things quietened down. It was a very pleasant evening and the wait afforded the opportunity to watch the rest of the wildlife using the feeding area. Pheasants and foxes and various small birds were scanning the site for morsels of food overlooked by the boar. Here I was perched 14 feet up a tree out of sight and all at peace then all of a sudden the birds and other wildlife upped and left in a hurry. I decided to give it another 10 minutes or so before descending and making my way back to my car which was some two miles away. Moments later I heard a female voice coming through the wood towards the sight, then a second voice belonging to a male.

Not wishing to give my position away in the forest, I decided to let this couple pass before leaving and so stayed where I was. It was unusual for people to make their way this far off the main track. The going was quite difficult what with broken branches and low stunted brambles covering the ground. The only clear area was that cleared by the boar rooting for my feed. This clear area was some 25 yards from my high seat. The ground between was covered in fallen branches so the only clear spot for quite some way was my feeding site. The owners of the two voices then came into view, a young couple, well young to me anyway;

when you are 60 plus every one looks young. This couple paused when they reached the clearing and stood looking at the sign of boar for a few moments then they embraced and began to disrobe. Oh what to do? I had no wish to give away the location of my high seat but I certainly had no desire to be a witness to what was about to happen. I decided a discreet cough may put a halt to proceedings. The startled couple glanced around for the source of the cough. They could see nothing but the interruption was enough for them to reconsider and clothing readjusted they swiftly made their way out of the wood. An embarrassing situation avoided, the location of my high seat undiscovered was a good outcome but I confess to a slight pang of guilt at having ruined a lovers' amorous moment. I left for home, I saw no boar that night but it had been mildly entertaining.

This new site tucked away as it was should, I hoped, give me a chance to film the boar in a more secure environment. An area open to the elements does seem to put the boar on edge all the time. There was plenty of permanent leaf cover above them and I hoped that they would act in a more natural way whilst on feed. Under the cover of the trees they seem to regard themselves as invisible and relax. I wanted to film the boar relaxing rather than just feeding. I wanted to find out more about the relationship between the various adults in the sounder and the relationship between the yearlings and the piglets from that year's farrowing. How would they react? Would they socialize? Would the yearlings take an aggressive attitude towards the piglets?

I also wanted to test something that arose in a conversation with a boar hunter from the continent. It seems that there are a few man-made substances to which wild boar are attracted. One of these is a veterinary product called Stockholm Tar used for a good many years in the treatment of injuries to animals. Most shepherds would not leave home without a jar of the stuff. It was a magic cure for cuts and abrasions, it cured foot rot and helped prevent fly strike. In fact it was generally looked upon as a cure all. I had been told that boar would spend ages coating themselves in the stuff. I didn't believe it for a second. How on earth could a wild animal such as a wild boar know of the beneficial properties of Stockholm Tar?

My passionate interest in wild boar has meant I have been the butt of many a practical joke masterminded by close friends and I thought that this was another one. They assured me it wasn't but I approached the matter with some caution. I was concerned that if I spread the stuff round the site it would almost certainly drive the boar away perhaps forever. If, on the other hand it was true and the boar were attracted to it then I may get some interesting footage. In the end I determined nothing ventured nothing gained. I thought, if it all goes tits up I can always move back to my original feed site.

So I purchased a tub of the stuff from the local agricultural merchant and decided to give it a try. By coincidence there was a programme on the television which showed how the stuff was made. The main ingredient was pine resin and to extract the tar from the pine roots, the pine wood is heated in a container. When the wood reaches a particular temperature the resin seeps out and can be collected. I chose a suitable tree within view of my high seat and painted some of this Tar on the trunk in several places. The following day was a Sunday and with the number of people around the forest at the weekend, it wasn't until the Monday evening that I looked at the tree again. I could not believe my eyes, all the tar had been rubbed away. The trunk was about 24 inches in diameter and had been rubbed clean. The only trace was in the deepest cracks in the bark. It had been warm when I applied the tar and some had run down the trunk and soaked into the ground and this had also been rooted up as well. Even the roots of the tree were now exposed. So it was true the boar were attracted to the stuff. I repeated the application the following night, and the result was the same, the boar loved it.

So now I had something besides food to attract the boar and what's more the chance to film the boar using the rubbing tree, as it had now become. At the same time I was also experimenting with different types of food from my usual mixture. I had a clear out of the freezer and once again found some items past their use by date, in this case mackerel, cod and sea bass fillets. I took them with me the next time I went to feed together with a spade to bury the fish. I did this at varying depths to see if the boar would find them. All the fish were dug up the same night even when frozen the boar's acute sense of smell found the buried goodies. Unfortunately it was still not light enough in the evenings to film and so I have no recordings of these activities. However, I now knew that the reputation wild boar have as nature's garbage disposal units is fully justified.

Colour variations

My objective now was to see if the animals that were coming into this new feeding area were the same family group as the ones I had filmed the year before. Identification would be difficult after not having seen them since I stopped filming the previous summer. Although boar are very similar in shape and size there is quite a difference in colour between the adults, from almost black to a creamy colour. The normal colour of the European wild boar is dark grey to black with a silvery sheen to the long guard hairs on the older animals. The main population of boar in my study area at this time were of the darker type but with the odd blonde animal showing up from time to time. The reason for this difference in colour, so I was informed by the man from the ministry is a regressive gene in the boar's ancestry, although the colour is different the blood tests carried out by the ministry show the blonde boar to be true wild boar, and the thought was that this colour variation could crop up at any time in the boar in this corner of the country. The dominant male at this time was a magnificent black animal about five years of age, getting on for four feet high at the shoulder and between six and seven feet in length. It had an estimated live weight of 200kg plus and most of the piglets born over the last few years had been of the darker colouration with just the odd light coloured piglet. This dominant male was shot in the run up to the rut by a hunter and when the animal was dressed out it tipped the scales at a touch over 400lbs, which would have given a live weight of nearer to 500lbs, as one chap put it "his head alone would have filled a wheelbarrow, he was huge".

Identification at a distance

Wild boar males can be difficult to identify from a distance, particularly in their first year. Whilst still growing and before they reach maturity, their shape is similar to the young females. Once the males reach maturity their shape becomes more defined and they take on the typical buffalo shape with heavy set shoulders tapering away towards a slimmer back end and tapering again towards the snout. The sows have a much rounder shape. They also have a triangular shape from shoulder to snout but not as pronounced as the males. The most obvious indicator as far as the males are concerned is of course the testicles but unlike the domestic boar the wild boar is less well endowed with the size and shape governed by the changing seasons. In the run up to the rut as testosterone levels rise so the testes begin to swell and become a prominent feature making identification that much easier from a distance. Once the rut is over and the hours of daylight become longer in the late spring, the testosterone levels fall and the males become less persistent in their pursuit of the females and at the same time their testes begin to shrink until they are almost invisible from a distance. By the middle of May the males lose interest altogether as the level of testosterone falls to its lowest point in the whole year. They now enter what is known as the anoestrus period, a prolonged period of sexual inactivity which varies in length from three to five months. This period of inactivity is specific to the wild boar and in some cases their close relatives though to a lesser degree. The domestic males on the other hand, due to selective breeding in order to produce an animal that the butcher wants, are not subject to such a dramatic fall in testosterone levels and their testes remain a familiar dominant feature to all who visit farm parks and children's farms. The dominant wild boar males will use this time of inactivity in isolation building up reserves of energy and putting on weight in preparation for the autumn when the whole business starts all over again.

Now that the alpha boar was no more there was a power struggle between the remaining males to see who was going to take his place, and the boar that won the contest so to speak was a light coloured boar about four years old, and he now fathered the next generation. The departing monarch must have mated with some of the older sows before he was killed because some of the older sows produced normal coloured piglets, whereas the sows covered by the new man about town were producing a mixture of dark and light youngsters. Sometimes a litter of piglets from a normal dark sow would have a light almost white one, and sometimes a light coloured sow would produce a mixture of dark and light piglets. Within the space of three years the colour changes would mean that the percentage went from 3 to 30% of pale youngsters and this is the same today. This regressive gene would be present in all the animals produced in this area and could crop up at any time and produce a blonde piglet no matter what the colour of the parents. When asked if this was specific to the boar in the south east, or all boar wherever they might be, the answer was that it was specific to this area only, and if light coloured boar turned up elsewhere we would know where they came from, and this would be a useful indication as to the spread of boar from the area of study, the light colour making them easier to spot as they moved through the woods. This also meant that it would be easier for the poachers to pick them out as well.

Murphy's law
Pigs of all kinds and in particular wild boar with their thick mat of hair suffer with skin parasites like ticks and lice, the rubbing tree I hoped would give me a better chance to identify the individual animals as they used the tree to try and rid themselves of these parasites. Identification was not the only reason for providing the boar with this facility, it would also

give me an opportunity to film the boar using the tree, or so I thought, it was one of two things that I was eager to get on film. The other was boar using a wallow. The wallows in this patch of woodland were all unapproachable on foot due to their location, the approach was through fairly dense cover and not one of them could be overlooked without giving away my presence. An alternative wallowing site needed to be found, one that could be overlooked from my high seat would be ideal. If the Stockholm Tar had worked on the tree why not a man made wallow, all I needed to do was dig a hole within sight of my high seat and let it fill up with water and the boar would do the rest, I thought to myself. I had forgotten one thing and that was Mr Murphy who always takes a hand in these things. The plan was put into operation one night when heavy rain was forecast over the next few days. The hole was dug to what I considered to be the right dimensions having not made a bath for a pig before it was all a bit hit and miss as to size, my thinking was that I could always make it bigger if need be. I need not have worried, the plan worked a treat, the rain came and filled the hole turning the whole thing into a muddy quagmire, perfect for any self respecting boar to wallow in, and they did just that, in numbers by the looks of the sign, but not whilst I was watching, and nor did they use the rubbing tree whilst I was watching either, now this is where Mr Murphy comes in.

I was unwell for a few days and asked a very good friend to feed the site for me and she agreed as always without hesitation, and asked if I wanted her to film what was happening on site at the same time, I had not asked her to undertake both feeding and filming in the first instance due to the distance she would have to carry the feed, add to that the weight of the camera gear and I thought it would be to much for her to handle. "No problem," she said, "I'll manage somehow." It was more important at this stage to maintain a regular supply of food for the boar to find each night than the need to film, the filming was a bonus, it was the feed that kept the boar coming into the site. The result of this was, that on the first night she filmed a sow using the wallow,

126

and on the second night she filmed a sow using the rubbing tree, and due to my incapacity I had missed them both. Such is life, the best laid plans etc. That the animals that were coming into the new site were the same animals that I had been filming the year before was clear, with the exception of one middle order sow that was missing, the rest were identifiable as the same sounder. The same order of dominance prevailed, the difference was that the piglets I had seen last year were now all grown up, which made it more difficult to identify them, their colour had changed as had their shape, some of their characteristics still showed through which helped to satisfy myself that these were indeed the youngsters from last year. There were only 10 of the 14 that I had seen before, the rest I assumed had fallen prey to the poachers over the winter, the same fate had befallen the missing sow no doubt. Of these 10 yearlings, as they were by now, six were female and four were male, the rest of the sounder was made up of five adult sows, the dominant sow was about four years old as was one of her sisters, the rest were a year younger. Three of the five adults looked to be heavily pregnant, the two remaining showed no sign of being so, the usual feeding pattern would soon emerge, the yearlings would come into the feed site ahead of the adult sows and attempt to gobble up as much of the food as possible before the sows got there. Once the sows arrived the youngsters' feeding would be curtailed, the sows driving the younger animals away from the food at every opportunity. Feeding as I was over a large area meant that all the members of the group managed to get some of the food, although most was consumed by the adult sows.

Stranger in camp
On one occasion the sows were first on scene, and after about 10 minutes they were joined by a strange boar that I had not seen before. As he drew near to the feed site the sows as one attacked him and drove him away, he disappeared through the wood at full tilt and the sows returned to the food and continued feeding in the normal way, until one sow gave a warning growl

and the rest stopped feeding and looked in the direction that the strange male had taken and there 45 yards away or there about was the intruder, another louder growl from the sows and the intruder accepted the fact that he was not welcome and left the scene. The interesting point about this is that they were quite willing to tolerate the presence of the yearling males but not the adult male that had tried to attach himself to the sounder, thereby posing a danger to their as yet unborn piglets.

This is a good example of the lengths that the sows will go to protect there piglets, putting their own safety at risk to ensure the safety of their offspring. Taking on an adult male in this way is no mean task as the tusks of an adult male are formidable weapons, and can and do, cause serious injury to anyone who gets too close, but then the sight of five females attacking at the same time would be enough to drive most men down the pub for the duration. About 10 minutes after this incident with the strange male, the rest of the sounder appeared on feed, the young females first, followed a short time later by the four males who were definitely on edge, constantly looking around on the lookout for danger, while the females continued to feed normally. There was a perceived tension in the group brought on by the presence of this intruder, and the unease seemed to affect the young males more than the females. This stranger was not the reigning alpha male that had been holding court during the rut but a newcomer on the lookout for a chance to mate, but the sows that were sexually receptive were already pregnant and so he would move on. His colouring was of the dark type whereas the alpha was blonde and quite a bit bigger, if the two had met I know who my money would have been on. The only reason this intruder would risk entering an area that was already occupied in this way was if the resident male had left the area for the summer.

About four days after this incident with the strange male the dominant female failed to come into feed, a sure sign that she was close to farrowing, and three nights later another sow failed to come to the feeding site, and four nights after that the third pregnant female was missing. The rest of the sounder continued to come in as normal, including the two adult sows that were not pregnant. After two weeks the dominant sow and her next in line returned to the feeding site but this time they had piglets with them, four with one sow and two with the other, and it was another three days before the third sow returned to the site and she too had two piglets. This third sow continued to feed with the rest of the sounder as normal for a week, and then she failed to turn up one night, and I never saw her or her piglets again. At about the same time that the sow failed to turn up to feed I noticed that one of the young females appeared to also be pregnant. She was the dominant yearling female and was always first on feed, this is unusual in that there were two sows in the sounder that were senior to her in the pecking order, and I would expect at least one if not both of them to be mated before the yearling, which is normally the way of things. For some reason this young female had jumped the queue, that she was pregnant was now quite clear, but she was about four weeks behind the others. This young sow and her fate is described elsewhere in the book so I will not go into any more detail than I have already.

The situation did however raise a few questions, why was this young sow the only one of last year's youngsters to breed? And why did none of the more senior sows breed as you would expect, they had bred the year before so why not this year? It was beginning to look as though the boar were controlling their own population by selectively breeding. In years of plenty all the adult sows breed, as was the case with this sounder, the results of last year's efforts were there to see in the form of the 10 yearlings that were present on the feed site, add to that the four that had fallen prey to the poachers' guns during the previous winter, gives a total of 14 piglets from a total of six breeding females which gives an average of 2.3 piglets per sow, and that in a year when natural food was abundant. Of the five sows that were left of the sounder this year only three had bred producing eight piglets between them which gives an average 1.6 piglets per sow, which is an awfully long way off the predicted average of four to five per sow, so clearly there was something going on here that did not add up. The predicted population explosion was not happening, it's true that the population increased steadily for the first few years of the boars' freedom, this steady increase peaked after nine years and numbers seemed to stay the same from then on, and now from the evidence before me it seemed that the boar were controlling their own numbers by selectively breeding.

Piglet numbers

Only the dominant sows were producing piglets each year, and the numbers seemed to be governed by the amount of food available to the females in the run up to the rut. The dominant sows would claim the largest part of the food available by virtue of their dominance and so on down the line. This would explain the difference in piglet numbers per sow in that the dominant sow would be in peak condition when going to the boar and thereby able to support a larger number of developing embryos than the sows below her in the pecking order who had not been able to reach the same level of fitness or condition. From the evidence before me it looked as though the boar were producing only as many piglets as the surrounding woodland could support, this theory is further supported by the fact that the boar numbers are constant, and there is no population surge as would be expected if the boar were not in some way limiting their own numbers. It benefits no one if there are more mouths to fill than food to put in them. This type of population control is something that can be seen in other animals, the most obvious is of course the wolf who control their numbers according to the amount of prey species available to them. The alpha pair decides who should breed and who should not, unauthorised pregnancy being punished by expulsion from the pack and almost certain death for the cubs. It is nature's way.

In the middle ages an area of woodland was valued not only by its timber content but also by the number of swine it could support, too many and they did not thrive, too few and they became over fat and reduced in value at the market, finding a happy medium was the key to success for both the swine and the landowner. When first asked by members of the media how many wild boar there were roaming free in my study area back in 1996/7, I replied that it was not possible to give an accurate figure, due mainly to the secretive nature of the boar themselves, and the fact that I did not have access to large areas of private land and therefore no knowledge of numbers on such land. My area of study was land in public ownership, i.e. Forestry Commission, and wildlife trust. My estimate for these areas at that time was 300 to 400, in the Kent and Sussex borders, this figure I would estimate to be about the same today. The boar are established in most of the woodland in this area in numbers that the woodland can sustain. Any surplus animals are either culled by hunters as they search for food outside their home range or the young males are driven out in their bachelor groups at the beginning of the rut, by the dominant male. The young males find it difficult to adjust to the sudden change in fortune that the onset of the rut produces, where once they had the security of the rest of the sounder to warn of danger, they were now on their own and wander from place to place looking for somewhere to settle. This inevitably brings them into conflict with other groups and with landowners who suddenly find that they have acquired additional unwanted mouths to feed, with the inevitable result, a freezer full of wild boar.

These bachelor males will be allowed back into the sounder once the rut is over or the females are either pregnant or "dormant" and the alpha male has moved on in search of more conquests. By dormant I mean when females come into season and are mated in the normal way but mating is not successful for whatever reason. Interestingly, when mating is not successful they do not return after three weeks as one may expect. These sows are always lower order sows, the dominant sow and her immediate successors are always the ones who produce offspring. Whether these dormant sows reabsorb the embryos or abort them I do not know. Since they produce no piglets they produce no milk, they cannot feed piglets as has been suggested by some. They do however act as baby sitters and child minders to the piglets produced by their superiors.

It now became clear just how far out the original estimates of boar numbers were. True if the boar had produced an average of four to five piglets each, once a year then the woods around the Kent and Sussex border area would be, after 12 years, bursting at the seems. Twenty years and they would need at least two more storeys to accommodate them all. This, in my view, provides good evidence that the boar are, in some way, controlling their own numbers. A strategic meeting of dominant females to decide who is going to produce piglets next season? Unlikely so the jury is out on this one.

So the struggle for dominance within the sounder is a very important issue. That females in their first year can produce piglets is fact provided the conditions are right. However, more often than not it will be their second season before they have their first litter again depending on conditions and their position within the sounder. It may well be that she will never produce any young at all in her entire life. One of the sounders within my study area consisted of seven adults and their offspring. In the best year the sounder consisted of 27 animals including piglets – seven sows, eight yearlings and 12 piglets. The piglets were the offspring of five of the adult sows, two of which had one piglet each, one had two, one had three and the dominant sow had five, the most piglets that I have seen in my study area to one sow. That all these youngsters survived and made it into adulthood is doubtful. There were two of the seven that did not produce any young that year and indeed one that never had any in all the eight years I studied that particular sounder. She still came in to feed with the rest as normal but was soon driven off the feed by other members of the group including the young males that were now a year old. Of the eight yearlings five were male and three female, again healthy looking young females over a year old and no piglets.

The following year the sounder had lost a number of members, all the yearling males were missing which is to be expected; they would have left the sounder in the autumn in search of their own sows. More likely the cause of these losses is that they finished up in someone's freezer. Two of the young females were missing and five of the piglets from the last year's crop were also absent. Six of the adult sows were there and the sow that was missing was one of the lower order sows that had produced one piglet the previous year.

The sow that was empty the year before was also still with the sounder. When they first came in to the feed site that year I thought that she was indeed "with pig". She looked so well and fit but again she apparently bore no piglets despite being missing from the feeding area for two weeks. I assumed that she would return to the fold with piglets, as the other sows had but she returned to feed alone and showed no sign of having piglets. Whether she did have a litter which for some reason had died or been cannibalised I don't know. Despite all the indications of being pregnant again there were no little ones to show for it.

TALES OF THE UNEXPECTED

The water cart

By the end of June into early July the undergrowth was at its maximum height and made filming very difficult. The summer heat made the ground very hard and difficult for the boar to root for food. Water in ponds and ditches was getting low and the boar tended to move out of the forest and into the surrounding farmland for the height of the summer to find both food and water. Food in the form of farm crops and water in the troughs for the farm livestock. So dependant are the boar on fresh water that one stockman found himself in an unenviable situation when he went to fill up the water trough in one field that was not connected to the mains. The transport used for this purpose is a farm trailer fitted with a bulk water tank which can be disconnected from the water tank and refilled at the farm. On this particular day the water pressure in the main was reduced due to maintenance work in the area and so it took longer than normal to fill the trailer. This meant that it was early evening before he returned to the field. There was still water in the trough so the sheep were in no danger of running out, in fact there would have been enough to last another day if necessary. On arrival at the water trough the chap had to dismount from the tractor to connect the pipe to the trailer It was at this moment that he had the feeling he was not alone. Turning round he was greeted with the sight of a group of wild boar approaching the water trough, no doubt attracted by the sound of the trough now filling up. More crucially, he noted too that he was cut off from the tractor. To get out of the way of the boar he was forced to climb on top of the water tank and there he had to stay until the boar had drunk their fill. In his words the drinking feat seemed to take forever. Although he felt intimidated by the presence of the boar especially as there were piglets present, the boar never showed any sign of aggression towards him and, once their thirst was satisfied, ambled away as though an encounter with humans was an everyday event. That the field was surrounded by woodland provided the boar with cover to within a few yards of the trough unseen.

Tales to tell

My time during these summer months was spent looking for sign and talking to people who had a tale to tell. One of these tales concerned a farmer from Aldington who was combining a field of wheat when he disturbed some sows and their piglets who had been laying up in the field. As the combine reached the end of the field the boar and piglets broke cover and made for the hedge some 45 yards away. He continued to turn at the end of the run for his return down the field when one of the sows, clearly having taken exception to being turned out of her hiding place, turned sharply and attacked the front wheel of the machine, gouging a lump of rubber from the tyre much to the surprise of the driver. He was safely in the cab and there he stayed until help arrived by which time the boar and their young had left anyway. There was the usual expected leg pulling among friends as to the amount of liquid he'd taken at lunch but the proof was there in the tusk marks on the tyre.

Another tale involved a friend and me as we were sitting in a chestnut coppice waiting for boar to come to a feed site. We knew from past experience that the boar did not tend to move until dusk at the earliest, if they had piglets with them they may wait until well after dark. On this occasion we were in position well before it got dark and the woodland had settled down again before the light started to fade.

We had been waiting for an hour and a half with the only sounds being rabbits as they moved from the wood into the field which joined the wood some 20 feet from where we were sitting. Their movements were given away by the sound of the dry chestnut leaves as they passed, almost a whisper in the quiet still night. There was not a breath of wind. The odd owl hooted in the distant conifer forest and a dog could be heard barking in the local village some mile and a half away. The whole countryside was at peace; then in the darkness we heard the unmistakable sound of wild boar some distance away and to our front. The boar could only approach the feed site by one route and that was to our front. The field to our rear, surrounded as it was by a new stock proof fence gave us the confidence that we would get to see the boar when they came to feed. After a further 30 minutes with no sign of the boar, there came the unmistakable sound of an unhappy digestive system, I turned to my companion rather abruptly and mouthed the words, "Was that you?" Quite certain that it must have been because I knew it was not me. At that precise moment a wild boar somewhere between us and the field growled a warning which was answered instantly by four more from all points of the compass, followed by the flight sound, a loud cough and then the sound of the whole sounder, piglets and all, rushing back the way they had come. They were calling to each other as they went. The piglets called to the adults for reassurance as they tried to keep up. My companion and I looked at each other in disbelief. We had been completely surrounded by the boar and had not heard a sound. They had even managed to get between us and the field which was only 20 feet away without us hearing a sound. Anyone who walks through the woods in the autumn when the leaves have fallen know how difficult it is not to make a noise. The night was still with no wind which would have helped to disguise our presence and only when the boar got to within a few feet of our location could our scent give the game away. Our movement certainly didn't because we had been perfectly still.

Boar ambush

On another occasion I was trying to find the laying up area of a new litter of piglets that I knew had been born in the area. Until now I had only caught a glimpse of the sow that was familiar to me, being a member of the sub-dominant sounder adjoining my feeding site. I had not, however, seen enough of her piglets to tell how many she had so I was keen to get closer to her to find out. I had a rough idea where she might be but that was all. Approaching the area from up wind so that my scent did not betray me was my plan and it worked. I got quite some way into the farrowing wood before I was noticed.

The first I knew that the boar were there was when I was challenged by a sow who appeared almost from thin air from a shallow depression. Her warning growl told me that I had been detected. Now this warning is normally followed by withdrawal but on this occasion she stood her ground, staring in my direction with her piglets around her feet. She took a step towards me. The right course of action under such a challenge is to back away slowly and not to look the animal in the eye. So retreat I did. Unfortunately the way I had come was now blocked by another sow, who had no doubt come to see what all the fuss was about. She too had piglets with her, so time for Plan B. I tried to move to my left away from the sows without causing them to spook. This was working quite well until I came upon the dominant sow from this sounder with her piglets. Now I had three of the adult sows from this sounder around me, one in front and one on each side. I knew that somewhere there was another sow and five yearlings, all I assumed within earshot. By now the sow I had first encountered had advanced towards me and as I retreated so she advanced, until I found myself backed up to the edge of the wood. At this point the wood was surrounded by a six foot high deer fence, and my only way out was over this fence. This would mean an act of trespass on my part and a detour of about two miles to get back into my feeding site but it was the lesser of two evils. I clambered over the fence and as I walked one of the members of the sounder kept pace with me on the inside of the fence until I was well out of the area.

Boar escort

I had been escorted out of the wood in this way before. One evening after successfully filming a group of yearlings in summer coat, I was making my way out of the forest and came upon a couple of sows and their piglets. They were using a wallow just off the main track. It was dusk and normally I would have been out of the wood by this time but on this occasion the boar I was filming had been late on feed and consequently late to leave. I tried to be out of the woods before it got too dark so as not to disturb the boar as I left. The sows were already on the move. The wallow was not visible from the track so I had no idea the sows were there until one of them growled. This growl was answered by another on the other side of the track. At this point in the forest the track is about 15 to 20 feet wide, and I still had about 300 yards to go to reach my car. I moved slowly toward the car – an alarmed sow will charge an intruder without warning if it feels threatened. The sows followed, keeping parallel with me all the while calling to each other until I was out of the wood. A wild boar escort for a wild boar fanatic, not many can claim that.

The boar that got his own back

Another wild boar story that raised a few eyebrows concerns not a free living wild boar but a boar that, up until this point, had been living the life of Riley with a constant and never ending supply of both food and, best of all, as many females as he could wish for. He was the dominant stock boar on a boar farm. Unfortunately age and fertility, or in this case the lack of, were beginning to show and it was thought by some that the old fellow was in fact beginning to lose his ability to father piglets. No one had had the courage to say so to the old fellow's face but piglet numbers were down, and with that profits. Management decided that it was time for a change at the top. A little bit of fresh blood would do the herd the power of good.

The decision was taken to purchase a suitable replacement from another boar farm that had eastern European breeding stock. Having had a good look at the possible candidates for this prestigious position, a magnificent black boar was chosen and the deal done. Now it was time for the resident male to be removed from the enclosure that he had ruled over for the last seven years. Easier said than done, this old fellah was not going quietly. To remove this dominant male, he first had to be found. The enclosure covered an area of 15 acres and, for the most part, was covered in woodland, with the occasional open area with wet spots that the boar used as wallows. Consequently they would often be knee deep or more immersed in mud, so much so that you could walk right past them and not know they were there. The secretive nature of these animals meant that even captive animals given this sort of extensive cover to hide in would be difficult and time-consuming to track down. So it was decided to let nature take its course, fight for dominance and survival of the fittest prevails in the wild so why not apply it in captivity as well .

The newcomer was duly released into the enclosure. It was expected that the newcomer would be quickly detected by the resident male and the ensuing power struggle would sort out who was to take over as stock boar. There was little doubt in the minds of the stockmen about the outcome, the newcomer, being far superior in size and condition to the resident male. The confrontation could be heard from some distance away and the sounds of combat grew ever closer to the enclosure main gates. The estate manager's office was only some 400 yards away and he decided to take a closer look. He drove down to the gateway where he parked. These gates were locked for security reasons required by the dangerous wild animal licence. He entered the enclosure, dutifully locked the gates behind him and proceeded to approach the sound of battle. Suddenly all went quiet. Now driven by his curiosity as to the final result, he moved further into the timbered area only to find himself pretty much face to face with the loser. The loser looked decidedly unhappy. After all he had just lost all the nooky he could ever want to a handsome beast from Russia. He was injured and a sore loser to boot. Whether the boar saw the Estate Manager as the prime perpetrator reason for his fall from grace and the time for revenge was now, the manager was not about analyse. This was one very angry boar and the words "Get out fast" reverberated in his head.

As luck would have it the chap was standing by a substantial tree with overhanging branches easily reached from the ground. He made it to safety with ease. Now all he had to do was contact one of the farm staff on his mobile to help him out of this predicament. Where was his mobile? Not in his pockets, he determined after a thorough search, it was in the car some 30 yards away. Shouting would not work because the staff were all working away from the enclosure. The boar gave no indication that he was ready to move from his position at the base of the tree. Why should he, he had no where else to go? No brutal revenge could be had right here.

It was the manager's wife who found him, still stuck up the tree, some three and a half hours later. When he failed to come home for tea she had raised the alarm. After the rescue was completed and the chap was once again outside of the enclosure, the entire staff were sworn to secrecy which is how the story came to me, in the strictest confidence!

Tusking posts and scent marking

One of the things I started to notice as I searched the woods for evidence of boar was tusk marks on young saplings up to about four feet from the ground. It was thought by some to be the boar marking his territory and that these were tusking trees or boundary markers. A fanciful notion I am afraid, the boar, being nomadic, do not mark their territory. They do not have scent glands on their tusks as has been suggested for the simple reason that the males' tusks continue to grow throughout their lives and are constantly ground against the teeth in the upper jaw to maintain a razor sharp edge to the lower tusks. So scent glands in the tusks can be ruled out. We can also rule out the scenting-post idea because if this were the case the post would be in constant use by every boar that passed by. This would mean that the marks would change every day and they do not. What is most likely is that the tusk marks which is what they are, come about by accident and are made not only by males but also by the females. The boar due to their constant rooting often get an accumulation of mud build up on their snouts. When this dries it becomes very uncomfortable and to get rid of the irritation they find a suitably sized sapling against which to rub their snouts. All these so called tusking posts, on closer inspection, show the tell tale sign of mud and shows that the marks have been made by different sized tusks and therefore animals. The boars' thick matted hair is also an issue for them and they are constantly seeking out communal rubbing posts to rid themselves of unwanted hair and more to the point unwanted parasites.

Foot and mouth outbreak

After two years of studying the boar came the worst outbreak of Foot and Mouth disease that the country has ever seen. The entire countryside was closed down and the rapid spread of the infection from north to south and east to west would mean that not only was the farming community affected but so to were the general public. Woods and forests were closed to the public for the duration. There were those of course who ignored this with little thought for the consequences of their actions. Rumours of boar being trapped and moved from the Kent and Sussex border to other parts of the country were common by people who themselves were ignoring the requests that ban walking the countryside, claimed to have seen boar being loaded into vehicles from trapping sites. This type of action by a selfish few not only broke the emergency restrictions but it also put at risk the entire farming industry in an area that did not have a problem with the disease. There were no cases of Foot and Mouth in this area of the country at that time, the nearest being some 60 odd miles away.

The ministry, on the other hand, it seems were not covered by the same rules as the rest of us and continued to visit the area on a regular basis citing the need to monitor the boar for signs of disease. Foolhardy you might think. Driving hundreds of miles across the country from infected areas to uninfected areas, seemed to me to be far too big a risk but then who am I to question. The fact that neither the operatives nor the vehicles were disinfected on entering or leaving the forest beggars belief. Pigs of all kinds are most susceptible to Foot and Mouth and wild boar in particular pose an even greater risk due to their nomadic nature.

Pigs of all kinds become carriers of the disease as soon as they are infected unlike other animals which have an incubation period of several days before they become contagious. The havoc that would have ensued in the south east corner of the country if the disease had been brought into the area doesn't bear thinking about. When the figures were released after the disease had been brought under control, no wild boar on boar farms had been culled. Good news for wild boar farming and shows it is as safe as can be as far as infection control is concerned. Given the number of boar farms scattered throughout the country, some in areas that were affected by the disease, it is nothing short of miraculous to think that none were affected.

This enforced lay off in my studies would mean that I would stand very little chance of recognising any of the animals when I resumed my studies the following year. Having missed an entire year's crop of youngsters would mean that I would not have a clue as to who was who. A set back I could have well done without, as no doubt could the entire agricultural community. My thinking was that in order to study the boar in a scientific way I would need to study the same family of animals year after year so as to get a true picture of their life style. For two years this had worked well, with the same animals moving into the feeding area at the same time of year. This shows that the boar remember an area as being productive as far as food is concerned at certain times of the year. Now after the enforced lay off, it would be interesting to see if the boar would still turn up once I started feeding again in the spring of 2002. I need not have worried, I started feeding at the end of February in the same way that I had in previous years. The first feed went down on a Saturday in the late afternoon and I stayed in the area until almost dark to deter any other wildlife from taking advantage of the free food. The following morning the site was clear, there was not a trace of the food that had been put down the day before. The boar had indeed remembered the site and the time of year almost to the day. The week before there was no evidence to suggest that the boar were even in the area let alone visiting the feed site, coincidence maybe? The site was again fed late in the afternoon and I left for home with my spirits lifted, I was indeed hopeful that the boar would return as they had before.

Pressures of work would mean that it would be a week before I could check the site again. The darker nights made it impossible for me to get to the site during the week and I was only able to feed at weekends. The site was always clean on a Saturday due to the fact that every other mouth in the wood had access. It would have been worrying if feed had still been on site as this would mean that the wood was empty of not only boar but everything else as well. The second weekend of feeding followed the same pattern as the first, with the same result. For certain the boar had remembered the site. This second weekend's result led me to hope that if the boar that were coming to feed, it might after all be the same family as had used the site two years ago. If so, it would almost certainly be the yearlings who would now be three years old with their offspring from the previous spring. I would have to wait and see. The lighter nights could not come fast enough as far as I was concerned.

Above: The view from the hill overlooking my first secure feed site. This view or one similar, was enjoyed by groups of boar watchers from all over the country. *Below:* Mixed group of yearling boar averaging around the 40 to 50kg mark, just the right size the hunters are looking for.

Above: Two senior sows ready to take on anything that threatens their piglets. *Below:* Dominant male European wild boar, the sort of animal you give a wide birth. The scar under his right eye is the result of a previous encounter.

Above: Not what you want to see if you are a wildlife watcher or naturalist. *Below:* The end of another piece of semi-mature coniferous woodland and the eviction of the birds and animals that lived there.

Above: Before the harvesters arrived. Beckley Forest, East Sussex, the refuge of the sounders of wild boar. *Below:* The same area of Beckley Forest after the harvesters had been at work for a week!

Above: The youngest piglets to come into the feeding site, no more than seven days old. We can be sure of the age by the length of time the sows have been absent from the feed site. Below: This area of rooting was a bed of silver weed on a woodland ride and extended for over 150 yards. After rain it was that difficult to walk through, even the boar avoided it.

Above: *Typical wild boar damage to old pasture in the search for earthworms. In this case the fields were too small to be viable and have been planted with trees. It will be returned to woodland in due course.*
Below: *This more unusual pattern of rooting came about by chance and shows how quickly boar exploit a situation. The field in question had been mown and the grass left in rows to rot down. Where there is rotting grass there are earthworms.*

Above: Wild boar trap door type used by poachers. *Below:* Wild boar trap of the type used by the ministry in East Sussex.

Above and Below: *Regular visitors to my wild boar feeding site, fox and Jay.*

Above: *A devoted wild boar sow and her three-week-old piglets. The colouration is not unusual, ministry tests show the boar are true wild boar.* **Below:** *Wild boar tagged as part of the ministry study.*

Above: Wild daffodil wood after the wild boar had visited in the autumn. *Below:* The same wood eighteen months later, a carpet of yellow.

Above: Wild boar sows and their cross-bred piglets, the male was a black Berkshire. *Below:* Boar's head trophy, photo taken in an auction house in Kent. The trophy came from France.

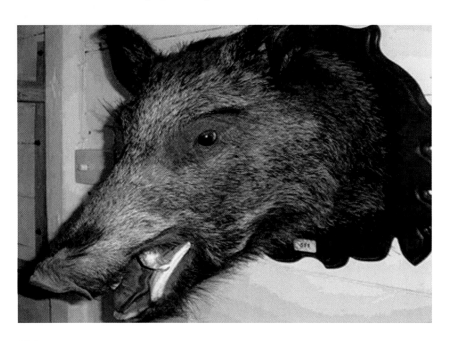

Chapter Five

A Fresh Start

THE BEGINNING of April 2002 was the first chance to find out just how many and which boar were using the feed site that had been so useful to me in the past. The restrictions brought about by the Foot and Mouth crisis closed the woods and forests to all legal activities including forest maintenance. The lack of legal activity meant an increase in illegal activity with the woods being visited almost on a nightly basis by one group or another especially if they held boar. As ever the perpetrators had keys to the woodland and the only clue that the woods had been visited was the fresh muddy tyre tracks left on the hard road the next morning. How many boar had been killed or removed alive for transportation to other parts I have no way of knowing. My hope was that there were sufficient animals left of the two sounders that had held my interest in 2000. It was a case of wait and see.

The man from the ministry was by now conspicuous by his absence and I heard through the grapevine that there was trouble at mill and that a new face would soon be taking over the survey. This change of operative was pretty neutral as far as my own studies were concerned. I had lost faith in the whole survey after the man from the ministry asked me on one occasion if I would explain the reason for making hay and silage and what was the difference between the two. If you are going to do a job, do it with pride and do your homework, I say. You just have to know your basics. This change of operative I would learn was quite normal in ministry departments; each successive operative starting from scratch, and each one refusing to recognise and build on the findings of his or her predecessor.

It is my strong belief that to study an animal at the top of the food chain such as wild boar it is necessary to stay with one known sounder and study them for as long as it takes to understand their behaviour and the effect that they have on their surroundings and the other creatures within the boar's home range. It seems the logical thing to do. Boar are boar wherever they are found but their behaviour may differ with circumstances and environment that bear little resemblance to that in this country. So studies by those undertaken in other parts of the world should be reviewed but not assumed to be necessarily relevant to the south east of England.

For a start the population density, numbers per square kilometre in the south east of England was, in the early days, higher than anywhere in Europe or indeed the rest of the world. With the areas of woodland available to them the boar were already under pressure before they really got started. This sort of population pressure had never been seen before so had no survey data with which to compare. So I can see no point in spouting facts that bear no relevance short of showing that the individual can read.

My data is based entirely on personal observations, on countless hours of hands-on study. I don't claim to know it all but feel I am justified in claiming to know more than most about Britain's population of wild boar, certainly that is in the south east. The situation in other parts of the country will vary with prevailing circumstances. Wildlife of all kinds is quick to adjust to different circumstances as they arise and soon learn to adapt.

With the lighter nights my chances of seeing boar on my chosen feeding site increased and by the middle of the second week of April I got my first sight of boar, the first sight that I had had for 18 months and a welcome sight it was. I had scattered feed and moved to an area on a rise some 75 yards away which overlooked the site. Being the early spring, the brambles and bracken were not yet intrusive and allowed observation without the boar being aware. Jessica my constant companion at that time, was the first to notice that the boar were on their way. I should perhaps explain that Jessica was my Jack Russell who always detected the boar long before I did, sometimes several minutes before the animals turned up. Jessica had the unusual ability to be able to sit quite still for long periods without making a sound. Most dogs begin to whine or fidget after a short while of inactivity, not Jessica. She would remain absolutely still and quiet until something caught her attention then she would look to me, wag her tail and turn her head in the direction of whatever it was that caught her attention. This sort of alertness was invaluable to me as with age my hearing was not as good as it once was. This early warning system gave me a chance to have a camera ready for the expected visitors.

The first boar to appear were yearlings and looked to be in good health, numbering seven in all. From where I was sited it was difficult to distinguish between male and female but there were at least seven animals that had survived the previous year's harassment. This first sighting lasted no more than a few minutes before the fading light indicated that it was time to leave and we crept away so as not to disturb, leaving them to clear up the rest of the food at their leisure. Over the next few days the pattern remained the same, I would feed, retire to the hill, check numbers as the boar arrived on site, looking to see if there were any new faces. Despite enjoying the solitude and peace that night time brings, I would leave before dark because I did not want to risk disturbing other boar that might be on their way into the feed site. The yearling boar tend to be a bit foolhardy when it comes to caution and let their stomachs rule their heads. The older the animals get the more streetwise they become and it was these boar that I did not want to put off because I was almost certain these animals were the remains of the sounders I had last seen in 2000.

Boar watching evenings

I now began to take note of the time the boar arrived on site and numbers. I had been contacted by various wildlife groups who were eager to be among the first to see free living wild boar so the pressure was on me to deliver the goods. If I knew what time the boar were likely to arrive, I could get my guests in position at least a half hour before to allow the woodland to settle down. The success or failure of this sort of operation depends entirely on the guests. The majority of people who are interested in wildlife are the sort of people who understand the need for quiet and are prepared to remain still and quiet so as not to alert the intended species of your presence. Just occasionally you get the odd one who disregards this to the detriment of their fellow watchers. One chap who after waiting, decided to record a running commentary for a friend who could not be with us, putting at risk the rest of the evening. A quiet word in his shell-like head recovered the situation. Overall I feel privileged to have met so many extremely nice people, all interested in my obsession. I pretty much had a captive audience. Of course it just may have been that without me they wouldn't have been able to find their way out of the woods and back to civilisation! I am pleased to say that the boar never let me down. There were occasions when the boar would arrive late and sometimes guests would arrive late and give me doubts about the success of the evening. Only one failed to fulfil my expectations, and for that I am disappointed. That disappointment was due entirely to a good deed on my behalf for a friend. I had loaned him some of my equipment for a project of his own and he failed to return it to me in time. This broke my 100% record. I still await the return of my equipment to this day.

The event in question was to try and set up a filming opportunity for a well known and highly respected presenter known for his outdoor activities. This filming was to take place towards the end of the summer which I had not tried before. My filming had always been in the spring and early summer when there were piglets around. By the end of June the undergrowth had grown to such a height that made filming almost impossible. So I would stop feeding the boar by the end of June beginning of July. When the phone call came towards the middle of September I was cautious and explained that this was something that I had not tried before at this time of the year due mostly to the fact that the boar tended to move out of the woods during the summer and did not return until the fruits of the forest started to fall. By this time there would be too much natural food available for the supplementary feed to have any effect. I was asked to try anyway.

To my surprise the first lot of food I put down was an immediate success and the next three days went the same way. I alerted the production company that I had at least eleven boar coming into feed but that they had better be quick before the acorns started to drop as this would spell the end of the boars' interest in supplementary feed. I was told that the presenter was in fact in America at that time and was not expected back in this country for at least three weeks. I was asked to continue feeding until then. I started to have doubts but did so just the same.

High seat in place and covered up as best I could the boar continued to come to feed every night until about four days before the date set for the filming. It was then that I found that not all the feed had been cleared up, a bad sign. I passed on my concerns to the filmers, "Not to worry we'll take a chance," I was told. Needless to say the night was unsuccessful, we never saw a single animal although we heard them in the oak woodland that bordered the feeding site. If we had been able to film three weeks sooner I am sure we would have been successful. This one failure will always be a regret of mine.

When first approached to arrange these boar watching evenings I was a little unsure what to expect, from the contact that I had it was quite obvious to me, and to the organizations that were involved, that there were far more people wanting to see the boar than I could safely cater for. Reluctantly I found it necessary to limit the number of people to seven at a time and, to preserve the safety of the boar, I also decided to limit the number of trips each year to six, after all my main reason for my activities was to study the wild boar in their natural environment, not to attract tourists. The first group of boar watchers arrived at the designated rendezvous on time, a good sign, a little apprehensive at first. I introduced myself and explained what I expected to see and a few things that I required from them in order for the evening to be successful. I asked that questions be kept to a minimum and be whispered at all times until after the boar had left the feeding site after which I would be pleased to answer all their questions as best I could. The evening could not have gone better, we arrived on site in good time. The evening was mild and humid and once everyone had settled down and got comfortable we waited quietly for the arrival of the boar.

Having explained in whispered tones on arrival at the feeding site, the direction I thought the boar would come from, and that I would appreciate them not using their cameras once the light started to fade (I thought the flash might spook the boar), we were all taken by surprise when the boar came in from a totally different direction. It was quite clear from their appearance that they had visited a wallow before coming in to feed.

The first two animals to appear arrived covered in mud. Coincident with their arrival the air temperature dropped and the mist started to rise in the hollows, the boar were appearing and disappearing back into the bank of mist as it drifted towards us and as if on cue the nightingales started to sing at the tops of their voices. A peacock, one of several on a local estate not too far away joined the ensemble, the sound sending shivers down the spine! The atmosphere in the forest had now turned decidedly medieval, perfect for the return of a medieval creature. It gave those present memories that they will never forget, myself included. The sounds of those nightingales perched on the highest branches of the pine trees, singing their hearts out as we left the forest, was beyond compare. To say that this could not have worked out better if it had been scripted would still be an understatement.

People were coming from all over the country to get a look at this latest recruit to the list of resident species in this country. One group of boar watchers came all the way from Newcastle. All young men, as keen as mustard, they were noting down bird song in their note books as we made our way to the viewing position to await the arrival of the boar. I went through my ritual of dos and don't s, the need for quiet, keeping their photography flash-free. Photos without flash were fine but boar eyesight is poor any way. Over the sort of distance we were from the boar they would not see us but a camera flash was unmissable and always put them to flight. All of them were carrying ruck sacks which I assumed would have perhaps a raincoat and liquid refreshment of some kind, the sort of stuff that you would take if you were going hiking. What I did not expect was the expensive photographic gear that appeared from each and every bag. They all had tripods, spotting scopes with adapters to fit video or still cameras, lense filters, the whole works, they must have spent thousands. The photos they took were amazing and put my efforts with a camera in the shade. Their total commitment to their hobby was a pleasure to see. They were I suppose the mammalian equivalent of twitchers. Their knowledge of the birds and animals around us were second to none, and without a doubt, would have put a good many so-called experts to shame.

Not all the watchers were as knowledgeable as the chaps from Newcastle. What they all shared was the desire to see the wild boar in their natural surroundings, roaming free in the British countryside.

Ages ranged from 12 years old right up to the oldest who was 90 and, so he told me when we got back to the vehicles at the end of the evening, had had two heart attacks in recent years. He was however, determined to do the same thing again the following year, fate willing.

One of the more memorable evenings involved a party of six female students. Now before the reader goes jumping to conclusions, the evening was memorable in so far as modern fashions were concerned.

Let me explain, it was a warm evening at the beginning of June when the girls arrived at the appointed meeting place. After the formalities were over, I diplomatically suggested that as it might turn chilly later they might want to bring a jumper or light top coat along with them, dressed as they were in body clinging tea shirts and hipster jeans, and leaving very little to the imagination. I then explained that we had about two and a half kilometres to walk to get to the feeding site and that we get to the site as early as we could. The boar had surprised me the night before and turned up early and I wanted to be there before them.

When we arrived there was no sign of the boar so I assumed that we were in good time. Wrong, as I soon found out. I left the girls on the viewing site while I made my way to put the feed down. To do this I had to make my way through an area of mature conifers and it was while doing this that I disturbed the sows and their piglets who were laying up in the pines close to the feeding site. They took off as fast as they could, and I feared that that was the last we would see of them that night. I put the food down anyway and made my way back up through the pines to the girls who had caught a glimpse of the sows and piglets as they ran off through the wood. I apologized for my clumsiness at having disturbed the boar and explained that it might be some while before the boar returned to the site and that we probably had a long wait. I thought to myself that we might not see the boar again that night, but I did not share that with the girls.

The girls stood watching the feeding site for quite some time before their legs began to ache and they started to look round for something to sit on. It's a curious thing, you don't notice this fatigue if your attention is held by something of interest, in my case wild boar. Thankfully the boar returned shortly after and we enjoyed the rest of the evening watching the sows and piglets as they went about the task of clearing up the food. In the end the whole evening was a great success and the girls went away quite happy at having seen what they came for, namely sows and piglets. One of the first questions asked by the ladies was always will we be able to see piglets? Whereas for the men who generally seemed more apprehensive it was, are we likely to see anything at all? When the piglets did appear, trotting along behind mum there was always an "Ah, how sweet" from the ladies.

Wild boar watching events were restricted to one a week, mostly at weekends. Saturdays were favourite as this allowed the visitors more time to relax and enjoy the evening without the worry of having to get home for work the following day, especially if they had a long drive home. Another reason for Saturdays was that the boar had, by the end of the week, got used to arriving on site earlier than they did on a Monday. This was due, I think, to the number of visitors with dogs that always flooded into the woods at weekends. By Saturday the boar would quite often arrive on site before seven o'clock in the evening giving the visitors more time to watch the animals in a relaxed state albeit from a distance. It also allowed for photographs to be taken with good light which added to the enjoyment and the memories.

By Monday evening the boar were always nervous and jumpy, and more importantly a lot later coming to feed. Sometimes it would be almost dark before they would show up. The added publicity in the media added to the number of people wanting to know what was going on. The men from the ministry were forbidden to talk to the media as part of their contracts of employment. All government employees are bound by the Official Secrets Act and one got the impression that even the colour of the loo paper could be a perceived threat to the nation. All questions were directed to the government press office for an official response which like all official statements, said absolutely nothing worthwhile. In the early days even when the various departments had video evidence, taken both by myself

163

and the ministry man in their possession to study, the official response was that the boar did not exist. Eventually after the first report by the first man from the ministry was published, the response changed from not there to the situation is being investigated. Brilliant, they had at last learned to read. The publication of this report led to more interest from the media, both national newspapers and television production companies were now keen to get in on the act. Almost weekly there would be a phone call from someone wanting to know what was what. With all this interest things sometimes got a bit hectic but I managed to keep up with demand even though at one time I had two interviews in one day as far as I was concerned the more people that knew the real story of the boar, the more people there would be on the side of the boar if the unthinkable were to happen. My fear was that the official survey would come to an abrupt end with a decision to eradicate the boar that now roamed freely across the countryside, not only here in the south east but reports from other areas suggested that the boar were also establishing viable breeding populations elsewhere. This was good news as far as I was concerned, the more boar there were out there the better, and the longer the situation went on the harder it would be to eradicate them.

Having studied the boar for several years the one thing that stood out was that the boar did not appreciate harassment or constant disturbance. When this sort of situation arose the boar would vacate an area and move to an area with less hassle, only moving back into an area again when the disturbance was past and peace and quiet had returned and they felt secure again. If the disturbance continued then the likelihood would be that the boar would not return at all on a permanent basis, but occasionally as they passed through on their way from one place to another. Any sudden act on behalf of the authorities to drive the boar to waiting marksmen would mean that the boar would disperse in all directions, thereby making the task several times more difficult than it had at first been. My hope was that knowing the speed that government departments worked, and the speed at which decisions were made could only be good news for the wild boar.

Another reason for restricting the numbers of visitors was to reduce the chance of the wrong type of people. By this I mean those who had an ulterior motive other than just a desire to watch the boar. For this reason I would only respond to enquiries from reputable organisations or people I knew and could trust to keep the location of the feeding site to themselves. My main fear was that the feeding site would be discovered by those who wished to use my efforts to study the boar for their own ends. After all there is always a market for wild boar meat no matter what time of year it is. That said I was always pleased to oblige people I knew as often as I could with last minute watching sessions. One evening a friend rang me just after I had returned from feeding. He asked if it would be possible to get a wheelchair and passenger in to the viewing site. I said I thought it totally out of the question. It was in the middle of a mature conifer plantation with fallen branches and dead wood littering the ground all laced together with stunted bramble and woodbine. The access was challenging for an able bodied individual let alone one in a wheelchair. Clearly determined, she asked if I would mind if she gave it a try. I had known the incapacitated person for years and told her I had no problems. I offered to help but she had it all worked out. Her family were going to assist, "We will also take in enough feed to keep the boar happy so you can have a night off," she told me. "Well I hope you know what you are doing," I replied adding that if they got into difficulty I was on the other end of the phone.

The appointed evening arrived and I waited by the phone sure that sooner or later I would be needed to help out. Not a bit of it, the event went of exactly as planned. Apparently a bit of a struggle getting him up into the high seat but it all worked out perfectly. The boar arrived on site with the bonus of deer on the feed site too, a roe doe and her twin calves. Deer and boar on the same site together was a first. The event could not have worked out better. "The gentleman for whom this had been staged had tears in his eyes when we went to get him down from the high seat my friend later told me. As was explained to me later it was something that he thought he would never get to see once he was confined to a wheelchair, having been a true countryman all his life the wild boar was one animal he thought he would never see, and this was his one wish. For him the roe doe and her young were the icing on the cake.

The main reason for all this effort was to enable me to study the boar in a natural environment where they felt at ease. The sounders that had been coming to feed on my sites previously, that is pre foot and mouth, had, I am pretty sure escaped more or less in tact from the attentions of the poachers. Piglet numbers were about what I would have expected judging by the amount of natural food available to the sows the previous autumn. During my 10 years of studying these two sounders in detail and other sounders in less detail the average number of piglets was never more than two to three piglets per adult breeding sow and that was after an exceptionally good year with the wood and forests full to the brim with natural food. I recall now how it seemed that every tree in the wood was loaded with fruits of one sort or another.

More often than not the piglet numbers would be much lower. It is the easiest thing in the world to look at a wild boar sow with a litter of six youngsters, multiply the six by the estimated number of sows in any given area and come up with a figure that is totally feasible, but at the same time wrong. Boar numbers on paper and numbers in reality are two different things. I have heard reports of sows being seen with as many as 10 piglets, and these reports come from reliable sources. The reality is that what has been seen is a sow baby sitting the youngsters while the rest of the sounder are off feeding elsewhere, even the wild boar need a rest from the kids sometimes. These sightings almost always involve piglets that are almost at the point of fending for themselves, this is usually eight to ten weeks.

166

Street wise wild boar

My own observations have shown that the older the sow gets the less likely she is to be seen with piglets at foot. By this I mean that she does not come into the feed sites with the rest of the younger less experienced females who tend to let their appetite and the chance of an easier meal rule their heads. I have found that by the time the sows have produced three litters they have learnt that a free meal is not always a safe one and they are more difficult to film. With the younger sows it is quite often the piglets who lead the cavalry charge on to the feeding area followed by the rest of the sounder. I have seen older sows standing back in the undergrowth watching and listening to the animals already on feed on one occasion for 45 minutes only to turn and walk away taking her piglets with her. She was at least four years of age if not more and was one of the sows that I had filmed when I first started to study the boar seriously. In the early days she came into feed with the rest quite happily, but a close encounter or two with hunters had changed her opinion of free feed and its benefit.

By the time the adults get to be this cautious it is rare to see them at all with sufficient light left to be able to identify them. They tend to stay concealed until after dark and only then do they venture out with their piglets. Wild boar are intelligent as are all members of the pig family and quickly learn what danger is. The rut is probably the only time that this caution is relaxed. The urge to reproduce overrides the need for caution. During all the time that I have spent studying the boar, I have only ever seen a true alpha male in daylight on two occasions. The first was in the late spring, I was watching a group of young well grown yearlings, when I noticed that they were all female except for one quite obvious male who spent his time, not feeding as the females were but constantly moving among the feeding females scenting the air and generally being a nuisance. He seemed to be interested in one female in particular and spent a lot of time chatting her up so to speak. Now he was quite a large male, I would estimate him to be about two years of age with a weight of probably, 85kg to 90kg, the females on the other hand were about half this weight.

The female he was paying most attention to was an almost white one. He to was very light in colour. I thought that this boar would probably be rewarded for his persistence until, that is, his dad turned up. Now this newcomer to the scene was half as big again as the resident male and of the same colouration. The resident male took one look at the newcomer raised his bristles in threat display whereupon the newcomer did the same. One look at the intruder in threat mode was enough to send the resident male off into the sunset without a blow being struck. I recognised the newcomer as a boar I had given the nickname Halo due to the fact that the long hair around his ears made it look as if he was wearing a halo. He then began to pursue the young blonde as had his predecessor, that is until his dad turned up. Now the tables were turned for this resident and he left straight away without a backwards glance.

The new man about town was at least 200kg, nearly four feet high at the shoulder, and getting on for seven feet in length. Now his approach was totally different, he just sidled up to the female and shielded her from the rest of the group allowing her to feed uninterrupted. The light by this time was fading and filming was now impossible. The next time I saw the group was four days later, there was no sign of any of the males, but the female showed all the signs of being mated, so it looked as though the old chap's tactics had worked.

One of the governing factors in the mating game as far as free living wild boar are concerned is the ability of these young females to support the weight of these alpha males during mating. This can mean that the older heavier males are restricted due to their weight to mating with the older larger sows who are strong enough to support them. This then gives the younger males a chance to become dads, that is as long as the alpha is not in the area. I never saw that particular male again. That the three males were related I have no doubt as all three showed the same characterisation of the long hair round their ears that had given rise to the nickname of Halo in the first place. Whether the youngster was mated by the old or young male I have no way of knowing although I like to think that age prevailed. The results would be there for all to see in the summer when the female produced her piglets. The second occasion was totally out of the blue, driving through a particularly boar-rich part of the Sussex countryside in the passenger seat of a friend's Land Rover we were confronted by a large dark coloured male who just stood in the middle of a narrow lane in front of us. His shoulders were level with the bonnet of the vehicle. The lane was not wide enough for us to drive around him so we just had to wait until he decided to move. This he did when another vehicle came from the opposite direction. The occupants of this other vehicle were a mother and her two teenage daughters who until then had not believed that there were any wild boar anyway. Needless to say they were now converts.

The spread of wild boar in the south east has been a gradual and steady one. From the initial escapes in the late eighties to the late nineties numbers increased steadily in small isolated pockets, in some cases boar were present for several years before their presence was noticed by the people on whose land the boar had taken up residence in. By the end of the nineties the numbers were at their highest in the Kent and Sussex border area and the animals migrated to other areas from here, north, south, east and west. There were reports coming in from as far north as the Medway towns and east as far as the countryside around Folkstone, south as far as Eastbourne and as far west as Horsham in West Sussex.

To attribute all these reported sightings to the original escapees would be wrong and it is widely accepted that they must have had some help in the form of other escapes from private collections or wildlife parks. We know for a fact that there was at least one other escape in east Kent by the tissue analysis conducted by the ministry man at the beginning of his study, and further rumours of a boar farm that went into liquidation losing several animals in the process would also have topped up the animals that were already roaming free, adding new blood in the process. An incident when a consignment of animals destined for an abattoir at Aldington crashed and the contents of the lorry ran of across the fields and disappeared into the woods would also have helped the boar to establish a viable colony. The heavily wooded area between Battle and Rye soon became occupied by boar that had moved out of the border areas of Peasmarsh and Beckley, and from there they moved on to the countryside around Tunbridge Wells, and from there onto Ashdown Forest and to Hayward Heath. Each time they moved on they left behind a small but viable breeding population. I was asked by a presenter for a BBC farming programme in 2000 what my predictions were as far as the spread of the boar population. I said in 10 years I thought there was a real possibility that every large area of woodland or forest would have a resident or nomadic population of free living wild boar, and that numbers would continue to increase until they were out of control. The first part of that statement has proved to be correct, there are boar in most of the wooded areas across the south east, and indeed the south as a whole. The second part of that statement however has proved not to be the case, numbers have not got out of hand. On the contrary, the countryside as a whole has managed to cope quite well with the newcomers.

There are a few people who see the boar as an asset and a way of making a bit of extra cash by charging people to shoot boar in a controlled way by ensuring that only surplus males are culled. The adult males make the biggest trophy heads and are the first choice of trophy hunters but taking out the biggest and best each time is not necessarily the right way to go. It might be right financially but not necessarily right as far as the welfare of the boar are concerned. This type of controlled management is most certainly the way to go, with adult breeding sows being spared the chop in favour of younger animals who produce a more palatable carcase for the freezer. That this self-imposed close season is right cannot be disputed but in order for it to be successful everyone needs to sing from the same hymn sheet. There are enough people out there keen to shoot a wild boar and if managed correctly, enough surplus boar to satisfy the demand provided it is managed correctly and by people who know enough about the boar in their area to decide how many animals can be safely culled without damaging the viability of the rest of the population. Too much harassment and the boar will move out of the area, maybe into an area that is not so well managed thereby defeating the object of the exercise, that is to maintain a healthy breeding population of boar. Getting the balance correct is the hard part, better to leave one too many, than to shoot one too many.

There is no reason why males should not be culled all the year round. In fact the males are at their best flavour-wise during the summer months when testosterone levels are at there lowest. The females on the other hand should not be culled between the end of February and the beginning of September when they could be either carrying piglets or feeding piglets. The problem with shooting young animals during the summer is that the young males are more difficult to identify. The unwritten shooting code says, if you can't identify the target with one hundred percent certainty do not take the shot. Enough said.

Throughout the years following the foot and mouth crisis my studies followed the same pattern as my earlier studies in respect of breeding in that those years following a heavy crop of natural food produced more piglets than years when natural food was scarce. The only difference was that the colouration of the sounders had changed due to the dominance of the light coloured males who had dominated the area for several years. The male gene being the dominant gene meant that a larger number of light coloured piglets were being born compared to the early years of the boars' freedom but this would soon change if a normally dark coloured male were to take over the mantle of king of the woods.

My retirement from full time work at the end of 2006 gave me the chance to catch up on all those jobs that I had been putting off for years. You know the sort of thing, I will do it when I get round to it. Well, now I had the time to get round to it. It also allowed me to devote more time to the study of the wild boar in my area and perhaps extend my research into other areas where I knew boar resided. My hope was that the spring of 2007 would see me following one sounder from farrowing right through to the rut in the autumn. Time had never been on my side whilst working but now I had ample. By the middle of July in previous years I had lost contact with the various family groups when they left the forest for the farmland and the abundance of food and water available to them. Now I hoped to change that. I reasoned that if I continued to feed the boar on the same site throughout the summer months then I should be able to film the youngsters right through to the change of coat and the loss of their stripes. The stripes start to fade once the piglets reach five or six months of age and by the time they reach eight months the stripes have gone completely. My retirement, I hoped would let me film this process. I had plenty of film of sows and piglets and also of yearlings. What I did not have was film of the youngsters in between. The extra time available to me would also mean that I could spend time with other groups of people with similar interests and to promote the cause of the boar and get more people on the side of the boar in other areas of the south east. Well that was my aim.

The first few months of the year went according to plan. I had been able to feed the site regularly from the end of February onwards and the boar had responded in a positive way from day one once again showing that the boar do remember a supplementary feeding area as well as a natural one. My thoughts at this stage were that if the boar were able to gain enough confidence in the site then I might be able to get them coming to feed in the afternoon before the clocks changed. The problem with this was that I had forgotten about the alpha male still being in the area and so things did not work out as I had hoped. The presence of the alpha male kept the sounder on its toes and they would not settle down until he had moved on.

By the end of April I had been contacted by a production company with a view to filming the wild boar for a popular wildlife series. This would require extra care and preparation on my part to get the boar on site to film. This was normally taken in my stride but on this occasion I was contacted out of the blue by another company who wanted to do the same thing, only a month or so earlier. It then emerged that this second contact had been sent my way by the Forestry Commission wildlife officer in whose area the site was situated. Due to family circumstances he was unable to oblige and had suggested that they contact me instead. My main concern was that the boar were as yet not coming to feed at anything like a regular time and the due date for filming with this first group was only 10 days off. The only thing I could do was throw as much food down as I could carry and hope that the boar obliged. On the appointed evening they did, after a fashion. It was almost dark before they turned up and rather than coming in from the expected direction, approached the site from behind us. At one stage we had boar all around us in the wood, appearing and disappearing in the gloom. First one side then the other. It could not have worked out better, the atmosphere was delightful and the film crew and presenter were mesmerised, just perfect.

Now my thoughts turned to the second scheduled filming session. If the boar had not started to appear on site at least an hour and a half sooner then the chance of this second session being successful were slim. As the day grew nearer I became more and more anxious and was on the point of calling the whole thing off just three days before they were due. The boar were still not coming to feed until late but I now knew why. A dog walker had taken to walking her dogs late in the afternoon and on into the evening, all six of them, and this was the reason the boar were late, waiting until the woodland settled down again before coming in to feed. I contacted the director of the film company and explained the situation, and left it up to her whether they wanted to go ahead or not. There was nothing else I could do and the ball was in their court.

The presenter was a particular favourite of mine, a person who I had admired for his down-to-earth approach to wildlife so I was keen for things to go right, after all they were coming a long way, a six and a half hour drive, to see the boar. I need not have worried, the boar appeared on site as if scripted with the presenter sitting in my high seat and the rest of the crew on the high ground overlooking the site. You could be forgiven for thinking that there was someone sitting out of camera range saying things like, enter boar left and cue piglets! Even when the woman and her dogs turned up on the main ride behind us the boar took no notice. If the filming session had been organized one day sooner it would not have happened, the boar were simply not settled enough.

Little did I know then that this would be my last chance to film wild boar on this site or indeed at all. Within days of filming the programme I was notified by the Forestry Commission that my permit was being suspended so as to allow a thinning operation to take place around this area to remove those trees that had reached "financial maturity". The operation I was told should take no more than six or seven weeks after which time I should be able to resume my study. They were to give me the all clear before resuming. The operation in fact took nearly eight months due to a combination of managerial issues within the Forestry Commission and mechanical problems on the contractor's side. The woods were in a terrible and distressed state from July right through to March the following year. Thankfully the buzzards that had nested for the second time in this particular area of forest had by now fully fledged youngsters and were not in danger. If it had not been for the intervention of the wildlife ranger this may not have been the case. The start of work was delayed at the insistence of the ranger to give the birds a chance to raise their chicks, fledge and leave the nest.

When the work started the sows with piglets moved out of the area. The constant noise and disturbance was too much for them so they left for quieter areas outside the forest, taking the rest of the sounder with them. I had seen this sort of exodus

174

before so the disappearance was not unusual, in fact it was to be expected at this time of the year. The boar always returned when things returned to normal. My frequent visits to the area during this "thinning operation" soon convinced me that the job would take a lot longer than expected so I resigned myself to having to abandon my study programme for that year. I fully expected the boar to stay away for the rest of the summer but I was sure they would return in time for the rut. This they did but the work was still going on in the forest, they left again within a couple of days. That was in 2007. In the spring of 2008 the sows returned to the farrowing areas but again the contractors were still in the woods and they too left for a quieter less hazardous piece of woodland.

By the autumn of the same year work was finally complete and the forest began to get back to normal. The deer had moved back in and so had the boar and I was optimistic that the following year would see the forest back to its normal self. The signs looked good, the amount of boar sign was what I would have expected to see anyway. With the rut under way by the middle of November there was the usual reports of lone males being seen in unusual places, dominant males had asked them to move out so to speak.

When I approached the forest authority for a permit for the forthcoming year I was told that there was the possibility that more harvesting operations were in the pipeline, and there would be a delay in the granting of permits. I visited the forest to find out what was going on. What had been a quiet peaceful area of forest with its population of owls, buzzards, sparrow hawks, knight-jars, gold-crests, fire-crests, and myriad other birds and animals that make up a thriving English woodland, now had nowhere to live. There were huge machines clear-felling the 100 foot high conifers that were so favoured by the owls and buzzards. Further there were large areas of chestnut coppice and birch being ground to pulp. As you can imagine the scene was one of total destruction. The noise from all this machinery could be heard a kilometre away, the tracks were chewed up and impassable. The reason for all this devastation? To attract butterflies and insects. The entomologists among you will no doubt be rubbing your hands at this news but I fear the bird watchers may not be so happy. To sit and listen to the five resident pairs of tawny owls declaring their territory on a still, mild evening is a delight and many others I am sure, represent the true sounds of an English wood. There were two pairs of buzzards who had raised young in the forest the previous year, the first to do so for a good many years. Their nesting sites were now nothing more than a pile of mashed up twigs. Where once there was forest there was now nothing but a smouldering heap of brush and branches on a burnt out fire. "What is it to be replanted with?" I asked. "Nothing," came the reply. It will be left to regenerate naturally which in this neck of the woods will mean birch scrub and bramble, the very stuff that had just been destroyed. This sort of clear felling was not only happening in my study area but all over the south east. Woodland rides and clearing tracks were being cut back to encourage the plants so populated by butterflies and moths and other insects. The

This is my patch, keep out!

thinking behind this devastation was that the woodland will eventually regenerate naturally and wildlife will return as before. But not in my life time. A tree takes many, many years to reach a height of one hundred feet but its life can be terminated in seconds by a chain saw. The boar were now forced out of their forest sanctuary into the surrounding areas of farmland and for the most part smaller patches of woodland. This in turn made them vulnerable to the attentions of others whose intentions were less than honourable. The wide open spaces left behind after the tree felling of their refuge is something that the boar detest and hence their reluctance to return. There will always be one or two animals who will visit the area from time to time but I fear it will be quite some time before they return in the numbers that were here before.

.

Chapter Six

Where do we go from here?

HAVING STATED elsewhere in the book that boar do not set out to hunt as a pack, I witnessed an incident that would, on the face of it, contradict this. I was watching a mixed group of yearlings and dormant sows on a feeding site one evening when the leader of the group turned her head and began to scent the air in a quite deliberate way. Then she turned and faced away from the site towards a large area of bracken some 70 or so yards away, scenting the air all the while. I might add that the wind was drifting from the bracken towards the feed site. She then began to move towards the patch of bracken in a most deliberate way, moving slowly and continually stopping to scent the air. She was now joined by two more of the dormant sows and one of the yearlings all of them scenting the air in the same way as the other had done. I had not seen this sort of behaviour before and I became curious to find out what had attracted their attention. Sitting as I was high up in a high seat I had a perfect view of the whole episode. The boar continued to advance towards the patch of bracken scenting the air all the time only by now they were line abreast with about two yards between them. When they got to within about 20 feet of the bracken they moved to surround it in a pincer-like movement whereupon a muntjac, the smallest of our deer species, broke cover and ran off through the adjacent conifers. The boar did not give chase as you would expect, but continued to investigate the area of bracken which covered about 50 to 60 square yards. That they had seen the deer depart was quite obvious from their behaviour, but they did not pursue. If the deer was not the object of their attention then what was? They had left an area of feed to follow their noses, for what reason? I have not seen this type of behaviour before or since. I cannot believe that they had not come across the scent of deer before because the area concerned had quite a few deer resident throughout the year including roe, fallow and muntjack. Why should this one cause the boar to behave in this way is a mystery. Was the deer a female? Did she have a fawn hidden in the bracken? Maybe that was the reason for the boars' interest. Another unanswered question to go with all the rest.

Whilst watching a group of yearling females feeding in the corner of a conifer plantation I became aware of movement behind the feeding boar, at the junction between the fir trees and the oak woodland behind. The movement was caused by a large dog fox who was moving away to the left of the boar and towards a thick patch of bramble beyond. The boar, as one, stopped feeding as soon as they caught the scent of the fox and moved to intercept the fox before he could reach the brambles. Finding himself cut off from his objective he retreated the way he had come but again the boar did not pursue. If any of the females had shown the least sign of having piglets then the behaviour would have been entirely understandable but they did not. They were all yearling females. This sort of behaviour by young boar acting together can only, in my opinion, be attributed to predator awareness. They were quite happy to let the fox go on his way as long as it was not towards the thicket. The fact that this area was used as a farrowing thicket may have something to do with it but I am not sure. If there were piglets in the thicket then the behaviour is understandable as the young females would then be acting as baby sitters which is quite normal. The thicket in question was so thick as to be impenetrable and I tended to leave these farrowing areas alone during the spring and summer months so as not to disturb the sows and piglets. Disturbance would, in most cases, lead to the sows moving out all together, in some cases taking the rest of the sounder with them. Far better to leave them alone. No confrontation no evacuation was my thinking.

Government involvement

In the years after the foot and mouth crisis the ministry operatives moved their activities away from their original research area at Peasmarsh and Beckley in East Sussex to an area south of Tunbridge Wells in Kent. This area at Bedgebury Forest near Goudhurst is the headquarters of Forest Enterprise for this part of the south east. This change of venue was forced upon them by the increase in interference with the ministry traps and equipment by poachers and to a greater degree by animal rights activists who were now interfering with everything they could, all things designed to make life as difficult as possible for the men from the ministry, at one stage the poachers were using the ministry traps to capture boar for themselves. The traps would be baited and set by the ministry men only to be visited by the poachers before dawn and the trapped animals removed before the men from the ministry had got out of bed. In some cases, it is believed, the boar were moved to other parts of the country alive with the aim of starting a breeding colony elsewhere. The ironic thing about this was that the ministry were providing the bait for the traps in the form of whole maize and the poachers were reaping the rewards in the form of either boar for the table or boar for transportation, either way it was easy money for very little effort.

For several years the Forest Enterprise press response was that there were no boar in the woods around Goudhurst and the world famous Pinetum but the gamekeepers and landowners were telling a different story. One lady in particular looked out through her patio doors and was amazed to see three boar in her garden, settled in the sand pit that had been built for her grandchildren to play in to be exact. Her property had a boundary fence with the forest which now incidentally had a large hole in it and was all the evidence that was needed as to from whence they had come. What also cast doubt on the denial was the rumour that forest rangers had shot 10 boar within the bounds of Bedgebury Forest, a rumour denied by the forest manager. No smoke without fire in this instance I say. Bedgebury now became the centre of attention as far as the bunny huggers were concerned and this made it necessary to move operations. This time the move was to the west country, Dorset first and then on to the Forest of Dean which had now become the hot spot for wild boar. From the first reported sighting of a wild boar on the outskirts of the forest back towards the end of the nineties when the forest was declared boar free to the end of 2005, the boar had, as I had predicted, got on with (you guessed it) what they do best, staying out of sight, avoiding contact with us humans, bred and increased in numbers to such an extent that they were now well and truly at home and determined to stay.

The release from a boar farm of a large number of animals of all ages during the winter months of 2006-7 caused immediate panic in the local press and the communities around Exmoor and a lot of publicity was generated by the attempts of the boar farmer to retrieve his lost animals. However, all that was achieved charging about on quad bikes and on horses and, at one time, a pack of hounds was exactly what the animal liberationists wanted. It was as if they had orchestrated the release and cut the fences in the first place. The hullabaloo guaranteed that Exmoor would now have its own breeding population of wild boar.

You see the timing of the pursuit could not have been better, coming as it did at the end of December. The sows would have been heavily pregnant. Sows on boar farms tend to become sexually active up to a month earlier than free living wild boar due to the high protein food that they receive in captivity, something that their free living cousins struggle to find. So by the end of December they are a month closer to farrowing than their free living relatives. Upon release the pregnant females would immediately seek to distance themselves from the area that had been home and find a secluded spot in which to have their young as far away from human contact as was possible. This is what made the deliberate release so successful from the boars' point of view.

A further deliberate release of animals from another boar farm in north Devon guaranteed the future of the wild boar population in the south west of England. Something that has yet to be explained to my satisfaction is how the animals that are now roaming free in the west country seem to have a small number of animals showing the same regressive tendency, colour wise, as the boar that are roaming free in the south east of England. Maybe the rumours that were going the rounds on the Kent and Sussex border during the foot and mouth crisis that boar were being trapped and transported to other parts of the country were more than just rumours. After all the regressive gene that caused this blonde colouration was, according to the ministry, specific to the Kent and Sussex area. To think that the boar had made the journey of several hundred miles without some help wants a bit of believing. How they got there is now not important, they are there and doing well by all accounts.

DEFRA research
In July 2005 DEFRA published a consultation document accompanied by two further booklets aimed at informing various public and charitable organisations throughout the country of the situation regarding wild boar. These documents included estimates of the numbers of boar roaming free and also predicted population increases and potential spread to other areas of the country. At the end of the main document was a question and answer section to be filled in and returned to the European Wildlife Division, Bristol. Of the 138 organisations consulted about two-thirds replied and the majority were in

favour of some form of managed control and again most were in favour of a close season to protect pregnant sows and their young. Some of those who replied wanted the boar eradicated including, surprisingly, organisations such as the National Gamekeepers Organisation. One would have assumed they would have been in favour of, indeed have welcomed another game species to boost the income for their membership at a time when competition from various sporting organisations made life difficult financially.

A close look at the documents and their assumptions shows why some organisations responded in the way they did. In order to make a decision about any subject we need to be in receipt of all the true facts and not misleading ones. The questionnaire was full of misleading information.

These responses were to be returned by the beginning of January 2006 where they would be appraised with a view to making recommendations to the Government about the future of the free living wild boar. A statement of findings and outlining proposals for going forward was to be made within six months. Six months passed and we were then told that the decision would be delayed until December. December came and passed and we were advised that a statement would now not be ready for publication until the autumn at the earliest. When the statement eventually came it did nothing more than confirm what we already knew:

(a) that the wild boar had escaped and established breeding colonies throughout the country.

(b) That the control of wild boar was to be left in the ands of those who owned the land on which the boar had set up home. The boar were to be classed as pest species due to their assumed danger to wildlife and habitat and threat to humans and their pets. There would not be a close season to protect pregnant sows and piglets. This was the only piece of information that caused concern. Where were the animal rights activists when this was announced.

The study had taken 12.5 years at a cost to the tax payer of close to £2.2 million. The conclusions for the most part were completely predictable and no different to the position that existed in 1997 when the study began. Disappointingly the report exaggerated the threat from boar and generally showed them in a poor light, as the villain of the peace. Just the sort of thing I had come to expect from these particular powers that be.

There are more people injured by domestic animals in a week, i.e. cats and dogs, than have even been threatened by boar in the whole of the time they have been at large. As for damage to the environment and the threat to the flora and fauna, more harm is done by man every day of his life, particularly by dog walkers not in control of their animals when in the countryside. The harm done to ground nesting birds and mammals is immeasurable. I have seen many instances of this irresponsible behaviour. There was one woman who would go home for her tea and come back later to collect her dogs. Hardly my idea of being in control. Are dogs being classed as pests, are there plans to ban cars? Cars injure more dogs and humans than boar do. Enough of my rant.

Included in the consultation document is a section on research into possible methods of controlling the predicted increase in numbers of wild boar. Note the word "predicted". After 12 years of intensive study they still do not know what is going on. All the evidence is there but they still do not see it. As the saying goes none so blind as those who do not wish to see. One of the suggested methods of controlling the boar numbers is contraception effected through a slow release hormone called Gonadotropin Releasing Hormone. This drug, once administered, would render the recipient, in this case the wild boar, infertile for two years or more.

The practicalities of capturing boar every two years to give them a booster was not on so a different means of administering the required amount of the drug was sought. The answer they came up with was to incorporate the drug in the feed on selective feeding sites and monitor results. A good idea you might think, but how do you ensure that the animals get the right dosage? An animal that is only 30 to 40kg in weight is going to need a different amount of the drug to an animal that is twice that weight. In a captive, controlled environment the drug did what it said on the tin and worked as predicted. In the real world you do not have such control. Boar being messy feeders anyway will leave spilt feed and the various other animals, domestic or otherwise, and birds, that have access to the feed in the same way would give the animals and birds the potential to feed on the contraceptive and all.

So a method of ensuring that boar were the only recipients of the drug was needed, a food that only wild boar would eat and everything else would leave alone. At one stage the food being used was the flesh from animals that had been killed as the result of road traffic accidents. Carcases were moved from the scene of the accident into the research area to see if the boar would feed on them. This information was common knowledge among people who work in the agricultural industry. How do you suppose the boar came to be called the agricultural garbage disposal system. Common sense tells you that if you feed flesh to an animal on a regular basis it will become used to it and will seek it out when the opportunity presents itself. They will actively hunt out animals like deer and lambs once they are returned to the wild. This avenue of research was thankfully abandoned once this became apparent to those concerned.

If a successful means of administering this drug to wild boar were to be found, it would straightaway have the potential to be used to control other species such as the exploding numbers of wild deer, now perceived to be a threat to the well being of the countryside. That the answer to the administration of the drug has not as yet been found is a blessing as far as I am concerned. I for one would not like to see a countryside devoid of new life in the spring. That anyone would even consider this type of population control I find very disturbing indeed. The quantity of drug required to render a wild sow infertile for two years would render a fox, badger, rabbit, hare, magpie, pheasant etc. infertile for life. Would we welcome that? Even the stalkers and hunting, shooting and fishing folk who manage our countryside so well maintaining the balance needed to sustain a rich haven for wildlife and for us to enjoy observing them would consider such control a step to far.

Another point to bear in mind is that this particular drug is also used in the pharmaceutical industry, in both infertility treatment and contraception in the human population. If the drug was introduced in some way to the UK countryside what is the potential for transmission into the meat of animals and entry to the food chain leading to undesirable consequences?

This sort of experiment with the wildlife in our countryside is wrong and the Government should take a much tighter framework within which Quangos responsible for such experiments are required to operate. Perhaps we should not be surprised by the naivety when we see so many recruited straight from university into these offices. What is needed is a balance of bright young things together with people who have been there and done it and have the scars to prove it. There is a famous quotation by King George VI which comes to mind and to me seems appropriate. It may even have been made with this sort of situation in mind. It reads:

The wildlife of today is not ours to dispose of as we please, we have it in trust. We must account for it to those who come after.

This says it all for me.

Diseases that affect wild boar

There are a large number of diseases that can affect wild boar and in some cases can be transmitted to humans. The most notable of these are bovine tuberculosis and anthrax. What is not generally known is that boar can also contract rabies and through direct contact with the saliva it too can be passed on to humans. Another is the lesser known Trichinella. Probably the best known of these diseases is of course foot and mouth, and swine fever. All of these can have a devastating effect on domestic cloven-hoofed livestock. These diseases if not notified and brought under control quickly can cost the agricultural industry millions of pounds and the loss of thousands of head of livestock. This is in my opinion just another reason why the wild boar should be brought under the hygiene regulations where carcases are subject to inspection by the authorities so that the animal can be traced back to its point of origin. But this risk seems to escape the notice of those in charge or it gets played down. Will it take an outbreak of e.coli or salmonella in the human population resulting from the unregistered sale of boar meat? Given the stringent hygiene regulations imposed on food destined for human consumption it seems absurd that wild boar carcases are excluded from such.

Age has now curtailed my wild boar study activities. This, and the clear felling of large areas of forest in my study area which has driven the boar out of their sanctuary. They do return on a regular basis to the area but usually on their way to somewhere else. No doubt given time the cleared areas will again provide enough cover to allow the boar to return in the numbers they were before but I fear that is some way off.

The future

Where do we go from here? With reports of wild boar sightings from all over the country, including Scotland and Wales and all points in between, eradication, it would seem, will be nigh on impossible. Management is the only sensible approach but by whom and under what regulations? Random culling of boar in one area may well help temporarily but will just move the problem on to someone else to deal with. Boar are extremely sensitive to harassment of any kind and move out of an area that is constantly being disturbed be it culling, dog walking or forest activities. Woodland that is disturbed on a daily basis by gamekeepers for example will not hold a viable boar population for long. They may well visit from time to time but they will not hang about.

As to the interaction of humans and boar in the Forest of Dean that has been widely reported in the national press, I can only think that such interaction is a recipe for disaster. Feeding boar at picnic sites has a detrimental effect on the boar in that they lose their fear of humans. Humans come to be seen as a source of food putting at risk anyone who walks their dog during the spring when piglets are at foot and the sows are at their most dangerous. Managed control of the boar around these areas should be the first priority of any cull programme. The boar around these areas are no doubt the boar that were deliberately released from the boar farms in the west country which would account for their lack of fear and also the fact that they are active during the daylight hours and look to these picnic sites as a source of easy food. I fear it is just a matter of time before someone gets injured by these over familiar animals. All the while they remain in close proximity to humans and their free handouts of fast food they will not behave naturally and will not return to the nocturnal ways displayed by their relatives in the south east of England. Boar that become over confident in the presence of humans should be culled.

If the boar are managed in the right way they become an asset to both the countryside and wildlife. They are not called nature's garbage disposal units and gardeners for nothing. Their rooting turns the soil in the same way a gardener turns the soil to aerate and dispose of unwanted soil-born pests and to plant the seeds that have been dropped by wild flowers such as bluebells and the all too rare wild daffodils. Their scavenging accounts for a large amount of carrion in the form of road kills and sick and injured birds and mammals like rabbits and pigeons. All are just a small part of the boars' diet. Better to take control now before things get out of hand than later when things are out of hand.

Fortunately there are a few forward thinking people who are trying to do what the Government should have done in the first place, that is to impose a close season in order to protect pregnant and lactating sows. Sows are the providers of next year's sport and should be protected in the same way the females of our main deer species are. There is no need to offer the same protection to the males. Bearing in mind that the rut is unpredictable as to its beginning and end it follows that the farrowing season will also be unpredictable and in most years protracted. These factors need to be taken into account when setting a self-imposed close season. Local conditions should give a fairly accurate indicator as to the start of the rut and therefore a date when you can expect the first piglets. With a rut that starts at the end of October you can expect piglets by the end of February and so on. This is not to say that the same time scale will apply throughout the country. Availability of food is the main governing factor so a year of plenty will trigger an early start to the rut whereas a scarcity of natural food will mean a delayed rut. It's not rocket science.

Without guidance in the form of legislation, it is always going to be a bit of a lottery from person to person as to when to stop shooting boar and when it is safe to start again without the risk of leaving orphaned piglets to fend for themselves. I am confident that there are enough responsible people out there to ensure the well-being of both the boar and the sport. At least I hope so!

If I was asked to suggest a close season to protect lactating or pregnant sows my thoughts would be February through to August inclusive for females and youngsters with no close season needed for males. I have described elsewhere in the book my reasons for this thinking.

My intention in writing this book has always been to try to show the wild boar in its true light and not as opponents would have us believe a bringer of doom. They do not attack humans and livestock unless provoked. They do not hunt down and devour new born lambs. They do not destroy acres and acres of agricultural crops. They do not triple in numbers each year. They do not breed all the year round.

And here are some other misconceptions to put to right. They do not multi-suckle another sow's piglets. They do not scent mark their territory, because they are nomadic and have no need to.

They do on the other hand cause damage to grass pastures in their search for minerals and salts and of course earthworms. They do turn over the soil in their search for grubs and bulbs at the same time aerating the soil and planting, inadvertently, large quantities of wild flower seeds. They do clear up a lot of carrion in the form of dead rabbits and road kills or wounded birds. They do seek isolation and not confrontation preferring their own company to that of others. Oh, and they don't fly nor do they ride bikes.

They will, if threatened, do what all animals do and that is defend themselves against all comers, especially when there are piglets about or, in the case of the males, females to be fought over. All that is needed to avoid confrontations of the boar kind is a modicum of common sense, especially in the spring when there are piglets about. Do not for example, allow dogs out of your sight when walking in woodland known to hold boar if you value your dog's health. If confronted by a wild boar back off if he doesn't and put your dogs on a lead. If the boar does not back off it is likely that it has something to defend so respect its space.

Simply rejoice in the fact that you have been privileged to see one of these iconic animals roaming free and unhindered in the Great British countryside in the 21st century.

Whether you be town or country dweller I hope you have enjoyed my book. I would like to think that one or more of you will have been as fascinated as I became in the life of these magnificent creatures. If this is the case then my book is not an end but the start of another adventure for someone else – a beginning upon which to build an even greater understanding of the wild boar in Britain.

Pursued again by the hunting men
Through the woods and the forest
They hunt again
For our heads on the wall
To be seen by all
Now the king is back in England

Three little pigs, the next generation